Kingmaker Power

The Legacy of Two Mothers

Kingmaker Power

The Legacy of Two Mothers

APPTE Publishing
1852 Somerton Pl
Virginia Beach
Virginia 23464

WELLINGTON BOONE

Kingmaker Power: The Legacy of Two Mothers

BISHOP WELLINGTON BOONE is a Christian author and researcher specializing in biblical worldview. He has been a pastor and bishop for more than 50 years. Researcher George Barna and Bishop Harry Jackson, Jr., named him the leading Black voice for reconciliation of the 20th Century. He has spoken for many organizations and served on many boards such as trustee of Regent University, which houses his collection of books, video, audio, and other printed materials. He has discipled generations of men and women who have become godly pastors and leaders with strong ministries and lifelong marriages. He is founder and chief prelate of Fellowship of International Churches and president of the Boone Foundation, a 501(c)(3). He and his wife Margarette love serving Jesus Christ together.

Wellington Boone's App, Social Media, and YouTube Channel

Website: https://www.WellingtonBoone.com/
Facebook.com/InternetBishop
Instagram.com/InternetBishop
Linkedin.com/in/Wellington-Boone
Twitter.com/BishopBoone
YouTube.com/NewHeightsNetwork
App: https://store.wellingtonboone.com/products/app-by-wellington-boone

CONTACT: Ministries@WellingtonBoone.com

Versions of the Bible Used in This Book
KJV Unless otherwise noted, Scriptures are from the *King James Version,* known as the *Authorized Version* (public domain).

Nouns and pronouns referring to Deity are capitalized unless included within a direct quotation, in which case original capitalization is retained.

APPTE Publishing, 1852 Somerton Place, Virginia Beach, VA 23464

Print Edition: ISBN: 978-0-9974710-2-1

The Adventure of Eternal Life

Imagine a journey that begins in the Garden of Eden and stretches into eternity, where mankind is not only restored to its original purpose but elevated to reign with Christ over the heavens.

This is not a fictional tale, but the ultimate reality revealed in Scripture.

While the children of Adam and Eve populated and stewarded the Earth, the spiritual children of Mary—those born again through faith in Jesus Christ—are destined to populate the heavens and rule with Christ forever.

This is the adventure of eternal life, a story of creation, redemption, and ultimate destiny.

Contents

Chapter 1

God's Just-Right Woman

None of us is perfect. God didn't make anybody perfect but Jesus, but let me tell you something right now: God is perfecting us, and the devil is not winning. You are made to win in life, period. When that Great Day comes, you are going to get rewards if you are not just enduring, but actively winning. Your stand in the Word of God, your dedicated prayer time, your powerful testimonies to others—all of it matters. You are being a blessing. There is something profoundly transformative about your life, your conversation, your thoughts, and your words when they align with the heart of God.

Listen to the realities of what God has ordained for you to be, and then walk in it! Walk in it in your thinking, in your conversation, and in your daily actions. You are ordained to be godly. Any other kind of behavior that you might adopt—getting angry at being mistreated, harboring bitterness because people have wronged you, or complaining about your earthly circumstances—that is not the real you. The real you is meant for dominion. The real you is dominating in this life. Jesus sent the Holy Ghost to make you conscious of the fact that you are called to walk in true spirituality.

The Kingmaker Legacy

We are stepping into a profound legacy—the Kingmaker legacy. As we look at the Scriptures where it all began, we must examine Genesis 1, 2, and 3. This triggers our thinking about what God said about the first Kingmaker, Eve, what Adam said about her, and then the woman herself speaking.

Furthermore, over in the New Testament is another Kingmaker whose name is Mary. Throughout this journey, we are going to talk about the distinction between these two women in the Bible—Eve and Mary—because there is something uniquely different about each of them, even though both were created by God with monumental assignments and responsibilities.

But right now, we need to go back to the beginning. We need to look at God's created order.

The Foundation of Human Existence

Let's begin by looking at the foundation of human existence in Genesis 1:26-28:

"And God said, Let us make man in our image, after our likeness: and let them have dominion over the fish of the sea, and over the fowl of the air, and over the cattle, and over all the earth, and over every creeping thing that creepeth upon the earth. So God created man in his own image, in the image of God created he him; male and female created he them. And God blessed them, and God said unto them, Be fruitful, and multiply, and replenish the earth, and subdue it: and have dominion over the fish of the sea, and over the fowl of the air, and over every living thing that moveth upon the earth."

Not Good for Man to Be Alone

Everyone on earth is descended from Adam and Eve. We are made in the image of God. Hear me clearly: the woman was not created as an afterthought. She was never intended to be an inferior being. She is the "just-right" woman, a helpmeet designed by the Creator of the universe for a specific, holy responsibility in God's kingdom.

Both the man and the woman were made by the handiwork of God, equipped to share in the divine assignment of dominion over the earth. God puts unmatched value on the woman, bringing her to the man to complete a unified, world-changing vision.

In Genesis chapter 2, verse 18, we see a monumental declaration from the Creator Himself:

"And the Lord God said, It is not good that the man should be alone; I will make him an help meet for him."

I do not know how many women have stopped to affirm that God was right about this creation. This is not just about one specific woman; this is about women in general. God is saying it is not good that man should be alone. He is not just talking about a male; He is talking about mankind. There is something fundamentally undone, something incomplete about mankind if the woman is not present.

The New Living Translation hits it right on:

"Then the Lord God said, 'It is not good for the man to be alone. I will make a helper who is just right for him.'"

This is a phenomenal point. First, she satisfies an eternal value in the perspective of God. With regard to the man whom God created in His image and in His likeness, God knew exactly what was required. He did not create a man in His image and likeness, as it says in Genesis 1:26, and then create a woman who was somehow inferior to that standard. Both were made by the masterful handiwork of God, and God determined that they would rule in this world together. Both are amazing because God made them.

God's Just-Right Woman for the Man

Let us zero in on that phrase from the New Living Translation: *"I will make a helper who is just right for him."*

There should be something absolutely amazing to every man about the woman whom God made for him. God has never changed His mind about the created order. God's original intent to bless a man with a woman who is just right for him remains as powerful and relevant today as it was in the Garden of Eden.

Many different men in this world have entirely missed this revelation. They have not thought of their wife as "just right" for them. They may think they have a wife who constantly corrects them, or a wife who asks for too much support in raising the children. In those instances of frustration, many men fail to say, "That woman is just right for me." But the Creator Himself says otherwise! He says, "I will make him a help meet for him." Just right for him!

Women Make the World Better

So let me say this directly to you women reading this right now: You are a just-right woman. You were created by God not just to make a man better, but to make the whole world better by the simple fact that God brought you into it. You have to let the Word of God transform how you see yourself. Men, you must let the Word transform how you see the "just-right" people God has placed in your life!

God could have multiplied the world in the same way that He brought Adam into the world. He did not need a woman to bring mankind into existence. God is the absolute source of all life in Himself. He does not need anybody else to bring anything into existence. He is the Creator, the uncreated One. He is the One who already existed before time began, so He is far greater than creation itself. He is the Great I Am. Every single thing that was brought into existence came from Someone who already existed, Who had no beginning, and Who will never have an end.

God did this exact thing with Jesus. He didn't need a natural process to bring the eternal Savior into the world; He did it by a Word that He was pregnant with from eternity past, and therefore spoke the God-Man into existence.

Where God Found the Perfect Mate for the Man

But for humanity, God chose a different, specific, beautiful design for creating a mate for the man. Let us look closely at the Scriptures again. Genesis 2:19-20 tells us:

"And out of the ground the Lord God formed every beast of the field, and every fowl of the air; and brought them unto Adam to see what he would call them: and whatsoever Adam

called every living creature, that was the name thereof. And Adam gave names to all cattle, and to the fowl of the air, and to every beast of the field; but for Adam there was not found an help meet for him."

Adam was made in the image of God. He was an absolute genius. No sin clouded his mind. He had the divine capacity to look at every creature God brought before him and name it perfectly. But in all that naming, in all that incredible earthly dominion, whatever God had made outside of the person of Adam was not suitable for him. Adam looked at it all and recognized, "Nope, not going to be it."

Then the Scripture announces a devastating reality: *"But for Adam there was not found an help meet for him."*

This helpmeet was not going to be like any other thing in the creation. She had to be of the same sort as Adam, but with a uniquely different responsibility. The very same God who said, "Let us make man in our image," also said, "I will make him an help meet for him." God said so.

She holds the same value. She holds the same creative purpose brought into existence that was solely in God's mind. No one else could do it. Only God could do it. And only God could give her this purpose. Anyone on earth today who tries to mediate or dictate your purpose outside of God's created order is lying to you. First and foremost, before any specific role regarding a husband, God was saying, "In the creation, I am making a woman that is going to be suitable for what I am doing in the whole planet."

You must get this revelation deep in your spirit, or you will miss the entire point of your existence. You are amazing. This is not to puff up your ego; it is to satisfy God's purpose, agreeing with the miraculous work that God did. The world will try to tear you down. People will try to say you are no good, or you are not smart enough, or you are not good-looking enough, or you have no authority. That is a lie from the pit of hell! You are the handiwork of Almighty God. And what God made you for, He is exactly right about it.

Bone of My Bones: The Miracle of Adam's Side

Nothing in the earth was able to meet the standard that God had set for this helpmeet. It had to come from something that matched the glorious creation God had placed in the man.

So, what does God do? Genesis 2:21-22 reveals the divine surgical procedure of the Creator:

"And the Lord God caused a deep sleep to fall upon Adam, and he slept: and he took one of his ribs, and closed up the flesh instead thereof; And the rib, which the Lord God had taken from man, made he a woman, and brought her unto the man."

Look at God at work here! This is purely God's doing. Some alternate translations suggest God took the entire side of the man to make the woman. This speaks to the creating presence of God and the unparalleled value He places on her. Do not measure your worth by a comparative value against someone else on the earth. Your worth is a created value given directly by God when He brought you into existence.

God didn't need to bring this new creation to the angels, or the cherubim, or the heavens. He brought her directly to the man. And look at Adam's response in verse 23:

"And Adam said, This is now bone of my bones, and flesh of my flesh: she shall be called Woman, because she was taken out of Man."

Equals in Perfection—A Breathtaking Couple

Adam was God's original masterpiece. So when Adam looked at this woman and declared, "She is flesh of my flesh. She is bone of my bones," he was looking at an absolute equal in perfection.

There were no mirrors in the Garden of Eden. Looking at the woman who came from him was the first time Adam saw in essence what he looked like! She was beautiful. She was gorgeous. And God did it. Can you imagine looking at the first woman whom God made? God makes man in His image, then makes a woman out of that man. Can you imagine what a breathtaking couple they must have been?

Their capabilities were limitless because there was no sin. They were absolute innovators in their competence. Adam had already demonstrated his brilliance by naming all the animals. Now, the woman was going to complete that creation, and the two of them were going to lead the entire earth together.

The Helpmeet's Calling: Becoming Like God

Genesis 2:22 clearly states that God *made* the woman and *brought* her to the man. She is the literal handiwork of God. God assigned the value to this woman and the value to the man. He told the woman, "I made you, and I brought you to the man."

So, all this modern talk where women feel they have to defensively shout, "I'm as good as a man! I'm smart too!" is unnecessary chatter. Why would you ever feel insecure about your position when God Himself meticulously formed you and brought you to the man? Why fuss about validation from society? God is the one who initiated the priorities of what was going to happen in creation. It was never your job to try and validate yourself. You were already eternally validated the moment God decided to make you!

Stop the worldly babble. Stop saying, "My husband doesn't make me happy. He doesn't spend enough time with me." When you do that, you are trying to govern how he should behave toward you based on worldly metrics of happiness. Instead, why don't you focus intensely on the helpmeet God has ordained you to be toward him? Don't you realize the spiritual power that carries?

You are the helpmeet, meaning that your very presence, your prayers, your godly character elevate his level. Instead of obsessing over how you are being treated in a fallen world, deal with how you were miraculously made and that your assignment is to be like God!

If you do not grasp this, you are going to lose out on eternal rewards. God has never changed His mind about the creation, the created order, and the created priorities.

God's Original Purpose for Creation

In fact, God's original purpose for creation in Genesis 1:26-28 has never shifted. He has only enlarged the periphery of it and expanded the competency of mankind in his assignment. By sending Jesus Christ, the Last Adam, God lifted our status from fallen human beings to eternal beings sealed with the Holy Ghost of promise! Nothing is going to be as capable as you are when you are God's inheritance. The power God gave Adam originally is magnified in Christ. It doesn't get lesser; it becomes greater through His legacy in you and your children, both natural and spiritual.

The difference now is that God gives you the power of choice. He gives you the power to choose to think the thoughts He thinks. He gives you the power to speak the words He speaks.

Life Is About Imaging God

"And God said, Let us make man in our image, after our likeness" (Genesis 1:26).

Life is far more than your daily problems. It is more than your circumstances with your grandchildren, your children, your husband, or your wife. Life is more than your job. You are more than all of that! But so often, we mistakenly believe that life is solely about our personal happiness. We think, "I love my family, I love my career, I just want to be happy."

Listen to me: Life is not about any of that worldly stuff. Life is about you imaging the Son of God, preparing for forever, and learning how to rule and reign with God starting right now! Ephesians 5:1 commands us to "Be ye therefore followers [imitators] of God, as dear children."

That is what life is about! It is not just about hearing a good sermon and thinking, "Man, God loves me." That is a retrograde mindset. It is not fundamentally about us—it is about God! It is about reflecting His glory in everything we do.

When you get alone with God in the mornings, don't just look for something special to satisfy your immediate emotional needs. Get alone, make yourself completely available, and let God initiate everything. What God wants to happen will happen. The priority of your life must be the availability of the eternal dimension in the exact way that God sees it. You are ordained to see creation the way God made creation, and then to function as a created being acting like God in the earth.

God's Decision to Give a Man a Just-Right Woman

There should be something absolutely amazing to every man about the woman whom God made for him. God has never changed His mind about the created order. God's original intent to bless a man with a woman who is just right for him remains as powerful and relevant today as it was in the Garden of Eden.

Men, you are called to understand and honor this divine order. Embrace your role in God's eternal plan and recognize the absolute genius of the helpmeet He has placed beside you. Women, step into the glorious, eternal calling of the just-right woman. Life is not about your temporary problems; it is about becoming like God and preparing for eternity together.

Questions for Meditation

1. In what ways have I allowed worldly definitions of worth to overshadow God's declaration that I am His "just-right" creation?

2. How does an understanding that God created the woman as a vital partner with equal value but a different assignment change the way I view marriage and male-female relationships in the Kingdom?

3. Am I currently focusing more on my temporary earthly circumstances and personal happiness, or on my eternal assignment to imitate God and exercise godly dominion?

4. Men: How can I better honor, value, and empower the "just-right" woman God has placed in my life, recognizing her as God's masterful handiwork?

5. Women: How can I shift my daily focus from seeking external validation to fully embracing my holy assignment as a powerful helpmeet and reflection of God's glory?

Call to Action

Reject worldly definitions of your worth and competitions in male-female relationships. Embrace your divine design as God's "just-right" creation, intentionally equipped to fulfill a holy assignment in your home and the world.

Chapter 2

God's Gift of Marriage

Marriage is one of God's greatest gifts—a covenant designed not just for companionship, but for reflecting His love, creativity, and Christlike character. I know firsthand the blessing and the journey marriage brings.

My first wife went home to the Lord after 48 years together; in that time, I learned how to blow her mind and even wrote books about it. When Margarette became my wife last June, it was as if God invited me to learn all over again. I found that there's always another level—new depths to pursue, new ways to cherish the wife God gives you.

Before the first marriage began, God created man and woman to be like Him: "Let us make man in our image, after our likeness" (Genesis 1:26). This first married couple would be like God. Their marriage would not be about temporary happiness or shallow compatibility. Marriage would be a union of two people made in God's image, reflecting His heart and preparing to fulfill destiny as they became one.

Too often, marriages get sidetracked by selfish pursuits or worldly values—looks, money, personal fulfillment—when

God's desire is unity, humility, and a love that puts the other person first.

When Adam saw the woman for the first time, he exclaimed in awe, "At last! This one is bone from my bone, and flesh from my flesh!" (Genesis 2:23). Adam honored her as God's finest work, naming her as the greatest gift in all creation.

Men, that is the spirit with which we're called to cherish our wives—not as accessories or obligations, but as treasures entrusted to us by the Lord. To cherish your wife is to honor yourself and God's design.

Adam also set the standard for our priorities:

"Therefore shall a man leave his father and his mother, and shall cleave unto his wife: and they shall be one flesh" (Genesis 2:24).

Cleaving Is an Active Pursuit

Cleaving is not passive; it's an active, daily pursuit—a commitment to make your wife your top priority, to hold fast to her through every season of life. In my experience, this means showing up with sacrificial love whether in joy or in hardship, and letting your actions declare, again and again, "You are God's gift to me."

There will be challenges. Sometimes, you'll need to pursue her heart anew, especially when disagreements or life's trials arise. Cleaving is about steady commitment, not waiting for your wife to change or everything to be easy. It's choosing her—every day—because that's the standard God established from creation. The world measures value with money or appearance, but heaven assigns value with love and faithfulness. Marriage is a foretaste of Christ's love for the Church, a vision to guard and pursue with all our hearts.

This is what it means to cleave and cherish. Whether you are at the beginning of your journey or decades in, God's invitation remains to make your wife your priority, love her intentionally, pursue her heart relentlessly, and let your marriage become a living reflection of heaven's love.

Questions for Meditation

1. Does my behavior show that my wife is my priority? What needs to change for her to feel covered?

2. In what specific ways can I more actively "cleave" (pursue, stick fast to, and cherish) my wife according to God's divine standard?

3. How does understanding created order change the way I view conflict and respect within marriage?

4. Are there areas where I have "stepped aside" instead of stepping up to take spiritual responsibility?

5. How will aligning my daily life and marriage with God's created order bring greater peace and dominion?

Call to Action

Husbands, take up the challenge to cleave to your wife with new passion and purpose. Overwhelm her with the sacrificial love of Christ. Wives, receive and affirm this love, joining together in the unity and blessing God designed from the beginning.

Chapter 3:

The Prototype of Eve and the Cost of Misalignment

We are stepping into profound territory right now. You have to open your spiritual ears and hear what the Spirit of God is saying to the church and to the family today. In this chapter, we are looking at the legacy of the original family, and specifically, the legacy of the original woman.

Eve is the mother of all living. She is the creative mother of all kingmakers. She is the prototype. But to understand her legacy, and to understand the condition of the world you are walking in right now, you have to understand the catastrophic cost of spiritual misalignment.

Catastrophic Cost of Spiritual Misalignment

Before the Fall, there was a perfect structure. There was absolute, flawless alignment with the Creator. In fact, before she was ever called Eve, she was simply Mrs. Adam. Look closely at the Scriptures. Genesis 5:2 declares:

"Male and female created he them; and blessed them, and called their name Adam, in the day when they were created."

They shared a corporate name. They shared a unified vision. They shared a divine assignment. She was the "just-right" woman, formed miraculously by the hand of Almighty God to fulfill a purpose that no other created being could accomplish.

But everything changed in the Garden of Eden. The Fall introduced disorder, and it fundamentally altered the trajectory of human history. It was not until after the devastating events in the Garden that her name was changed. Genesis 3:20 tells us:

"And Adam called his wife's name Eve; because she was the mother of all living."

She became the mother of all living but let me tell you the hard truth: because of the Fall, she became the mother of all living *sinners*. The seed of sin was passed down generationally. She experienced firsthand the heartache and the crushing consequence of Adam's abdication when he failed to maintain his original responsibility. As a result, the entire created order was thrown into chaos.

To fully grasp what was lost, and what God expects from us today, we have to look at how intentionally God designed this partnership in the first place. We must look at the divine blueprint before the misalignment occurred.

The Intentionality of "ASAH"

We have lost the revelation of how intentional God was in creating the man and the woman. God did not throw humanity together haphazardly. He is the pre-existing One, the Creator of the universe, and His design is flawless.

Let me give you a powerful revelation from the original Hebrew text. In Genesis 1:26, God says, *"Let us make man in our image, after our likeness."* The Hebrew word used there for "make" is *ASAH*. It is a word of divine craftsmanship, intention, and power.

Now, look at Genesis 2:18, when God determines to create the woman: *"And the Lord God said, It is not good that the man should be alone; I will make him an help meet for him."*

The word used for "make" in this verse is the same Hebrew word: *ASAH*.

Listen to me closely! The very same God who used His divine power to *ASAH* the man used that identical divine power to *ASAH* the woman. She was created with the same value. She was formed by the same power. She holds the same original, creative weight in the mind of God as the man! She is superior to all the animals, standing shoulder to shoulder with Adam in her worth.

Unique Responsibilities in Created Order

However, while they possessed equal value, they were given strictly distinct responsibilities. Adam was given the vision and the responsibility for the planet. The woman was given the responsibility to consummate creation, to complement the man, and to validate his leadership by standing beside him as his helpmeet.

The modern world hates this created order. Society wants to blur the lines, erase the distinctions, and tear down the beautiful boundaries God established. We see a lessening of devotion to biblical principles everywhere we look. Believers who once stood strong for the truth of God's Word are now bowing down to cultural pressures. People are terrified of cancel culture. They want to keep their jobs, their social standing, and their peace and comfort, so they stay quiet about the principles of the Kingdom.

What are you quiet for? Why are you holding back the truth? Thirty years ago, the proclamations of God were so strong coming from believers that the ungodly were quiet about their sin! Now, the ungodly are loud, and the righteous have gone silent just to survive.

You must remember that God is your ultimate Judge. The One who will judge you ultimately in eternity is the One you must devote yourself to presently, right now. Yes, upholding biblical principles—like the clear distinction between male and female, and the order of the family—will cost you something in this world. But the cost of compromising the truth is infinitely higher. Reignite your devotion to God's principles! Face today's challenges with unshakeable courage. Stand on the *ASAH* creation of God and do not apologize for His design.

The Abdication and the Shift in Responsibility

God set up the perfect order, but Adam dropped the ball. When the serpent entered the garden, Adam was standing right there, but he stepped aside instead of stepping up. He allowed his wife to fend for herself against evil. He relinquished his authority.

When a man abdicates his God-given spiritual responsibility, it does not mean the responsibility disappears. It simply means someone else has to pick up the burden, and that shift causes a profound misalignment in the home.

We see the immediate, tragic result of Adam's abdication in the very next chapter. Look at Genesis 4:1-2:

"And Adam knew Eve his wife; and she conceived, and bare Cain, and said, I have gotten a man from the Lord. And she again bare his brother Abel."

Did you catch that? Read it again. Who named the children? Eve named the children!

You have to understand the spiritual significance of naming in the Bible. The power to name is the power of authority. The name defines the responsibility.

When God created the earth, He brought all the animals to Adam to see what he would call them. Adam named the livestock. Adam named the birds. Adam named every beast of the field. After God created the woman from Adam's rib, Adam looked at her and said, *"She shall be called Woman, because she was taken out of Man."* Even after the Fall, it was Adam who called his wife's name Eve.

Failure to Exercise God-Given Authority

Adam was the namer. That was his assignment. But now, in Genesis 4, a massive shift has taken place. Adam did not maintain the responsibility he was originally given. Because the man failed to exercise his authority, the woman stepped in and took the responsibility. She named Cain. She named Abel.

When a husband loses his spiritual voice, his wife is forced to carry a weight she was never designed to bear. The responsibility for the family, for the alignment, and for the spiritual covering is meant to flow through the man. When the man is irresponsible, the entire family structure is misaligned, and it grows in irresponsibility.

Eve was navigating the pain of a world now deeply marked by disorder. She was living out the consequences of a broken structure. Yet, in His mercy, God continued to use this family to populate the earth. Eve became the prototype. She set a standard for all who would walk after her, bearing the incredible burden of populating the physical earth alongside a husband who had compromised his original mandate.

Two Realms of Population

There are two distinct realms of population we see in the Scriptures.

> **Eve, the first mother**, populated the physical earth with a husband through the natural seed.
>
> **Mary, the New Testament mother**, populated the heavens through divine revelation and the overshadowing of the Holy Ghost!

But everything traces back to this original misalignment in the garden. Because Adam abandoned his post, sin ran rampant, and the condition of the world rapidly deteriorated.

A World Corrupted by Irresponsibility

When mankind completely abandons its spiritual responsibility, corruption fills the earth. We see the horrific escalation of this in Genesis 6. The generational transmission of sin, sparked by Adam's failure, reached a boiling point.

Genesis 6:11-12 tells us the grim reality of a world without godly alignment:

"The earth also was corrupt before God, and the earth was filled with violence. And God looked upon the earth, and, behold, it was corrupt; for all flesh had corrupted his way upon the earth."

This is the ultimate cost of misalignment. When the family breaks down, the society breaks down. When the men stop leading, violence and corruption take over the streets. The earth became a toxic wasteland of rebellion because the created order had been totally abandoned. The people of the earth were entirely fleshly, completely disconnected from the spiritual mandate God had given in the beginning.

God saw that the wickedness of man was great. He saw that every imagination of the thoughts of man's heart was only evil continually. And God decided He was going to wipe out the corruption.

But right in the middle of this dark, depraved, violent world, God found a man who had not compromised. God found a man who understood the created order and took his spiritual responsibility seriously.

The Noah Contrast: Righteous Obedience

Contrast Noah's extraordinary life with Adam's failure in the garden. Look at the record of this man in Genesis 6:9:

"These are the generations of Noah: Noah was a just man and perfect in his generations, and Noah walked with God."

You have to make a note of that! In the New Living Translation, it says Noah was *"the only blameless person living on earth at the time, and he walked in close fellowship with God."*

Noah was a righteous man. While the rest of the world was giving in to their fleshly desires, while every other family was living in rebellion against the Creator, Noah maintained his alignment with God's design. He walked in the Spirit!

Because Noah took his rightful place in the created order, God could trust him with the vision to save humanity. Look at how God interacts with him in Genesis 6:13-14:

"And God said unto Noah, The end of all flesh is come before me; for the earth is filled with violence through them; and, behold, I will destroy them with the earth. Make thee an ark of gopher wood."

Notice the structure here. The Bible says, "God said to Noah." He did not say it to Noah and his wife. He did not say it to Noah's sons. God spoke directly to the man! The man is the priority of the created order. God established His covenant with the head of the household because Noah was positioned to receive it.

A Staggering Responsibility and the Testimony of a True Leader

God tells Noah a flood is coming to destroy the earth. He gives Noah the exact blueprint for the ark. He tells him to bring his wife, his sons, and his sons' wives into the boat to keep them alive. He gives him the staggering responsibility of gathering the animals and the food.

And what is Noah's response? Does he abdicate? Does he step aside? Does he question God's authority as Adam allowed the serpent to do? Absolutely not!

Genesis 6:22 delivers one of the most powerful testimonies of leadership in the entire Bible:

"Thus did Noah; according to all that God commanded him, so did he."

This Is What Spiritual Responsibility Looks Like

Noah did everything exactly as God commanded him! This is what spiritual responsibility looks like. Noah heard from heaven, he took the vision to his family, and he led his household to safety. He saved his wife, and he saved his children, because he was walking in close fellowship with his Creator.

Men, is that you? Do you have any idea what God has commanded you to do? What are you living for if you do not know the specific will of God for your family? You cannot lead your home if you are not walking in close fellowship with the Lord. You have to get on your knees. You have to seek God. You have to take your spiritual responsibility seriously so you can hear the voice of heaven and protect your family from the flood of corruption in this modern world!

Stop Asking God to Come Down. Go Up!

When we get distracted by our earthly circumstances, we completely miss the eternal perspective. People come to church, and they beg God to "come down" and hit their emotions or fix their temporary problems. They want an experience. They want to feel His presence in their flesh.

But I am telling you today, He already came down! He came down in the body of His Son, Jesus Christ, and then He came down again in the power of the Holy Ghost! Stop asking Him to come down to your fleshly level and start coming up to His spiritual level.

Galatians 5:16 commands us: *"This I say then, Walk in the Spirit, and ye shall not fulfil the lust of the flesh."*

He is already in you! Christ in you, the hope of glory, You do not need a new emotional thrill; you need to acknowledge the reality of what God has already placed inside of you.

Philemon 1:6 says that your faith becomes effectual by the acknowledging of every good thing which is in you in Christ Jesus.

You have to wake up every morning and acknowledge: "I have the mind of Christ. I am walking in the Spirit. I have divine authority over my home. I am aligned with the created order!"

Life is more than your problems. Let me say that again so it sinks deep into your spirit. Life is more than your financial struggles. You are more than your circumstances with your children, your spouse, or your grandchildren. Life is not about trying to find a little bit of happiness in a fallen world.

Life is about imaging the Son of God and preparing for forever.

You Are in Eternity Training Right Now

If you are born again, you don't have to wait until you die to become heavenly. You are already in eternity training. You can ascend into the heavenlies right now through the power of prayer. When you get alone with God and intercede, you are fellowshipping at the throne of grace. You are being changed, day by day, moment by moment, into the glorious image of Jesus Christ.

There should be continuous growth in your spiritual life. You should not look in the spiritual mirror today and see the same person you were a year ago. You should be putting on spiritual weight. You should be retaining the nutrients of the Word of God so that the anointing on your life breaks every yoke of bondage in your family.

Legacy of Two Mothers—Eve and Mary

Eve's legacy as the prototype and the mother of all living is a profound reminder of both the beauty of God's original design and the devastating cost of stepping out of alignment. Adam's failure cast a long, dark shadow over the earth, placing a burden on the woman she was never meant to carry alone. But the story does not end there. Through men like Noah, who modeled righteous obedience, and ultimately through Mary's yieldedness, Jesus Christ, the Last Adam, God made a way to restore the perfect order.

The Apostle Paul declares in Galatians 2:20: *"I am crucified with Christ: nevertheless I live; yet not I, but Christ liveth in me: and the life which I now live in the flesh I live by the faith of the Son of God, who loved me, and gave himself for me."*

Your old life of irresponsibility ended the day you were born again. Your old life of compromise, of fear, of fleshly desires—it was nailed to the cross! Now, Christ lives in you. You have the power to walk in the Spirit. You have the power to maintain the created order in your home. You have the power to cast down the imaginations of the enemy and protect the garden of your mind and your family.

Wives, follow the creative order. Encourage your husbands to seek the Lord. Tell him, "I need you to seek God so you know His will for our family, and I will follow you." Submit to the godly vision God pours into your home. That is a great and holy responsibility, and it brings absolute delight to the heart of the Creator.

Husbands, take your rightful place. Do not let your wife carry the spiritual burden of naming and leading because you are too distracted, too tired, or too passive to do the work. Get alone with God. Get the substance of what it takes to build a case for God in your household.

We are not playing games. We are building a legacy. We are raising up generations of kingmakers who will shake the gates of hell and populate the heavens! Return to the original blueprint. Stand firm in your faith. Image the Son in everything you do and watch how the transforming power of Almighty God moves from your home all the way into eternity!

Questions for Meditation

1. Have I fully grasped the intentionality of God's *ASAH* creation, recognizing that man and woman share equal value but hold distinct, divine responsibilities?

2. In my own family dynamics, is there a "shift in responsibility" occurring where someone is carrying a burden they were never designed to carry because another has abdicated their role?

3. Am I living like Noah—blameless, obedient, and walking in close fellowship with God—even when the culture around me is corrupt and completely out of alignment?

4. Do I spend more time focusing on my temporary earthly problems, or am I actively dedicating my life to "imaging the Son" and preparing for eternity?

5. What specific steps must I take today to stop asking God to "come down" to my fleshly level, and instead rise up to walk daily in the Spirit?

Call to Action

Take a hard, honest look at the “garden” of your own life right now—evaluate your heart, your thought patterns, and the principles governing your family. Repent of any areas where you have allowed misalignment, passivity, or cultural compromise to take root. Acknowledge Christ within you today, step boldly into your God-given spiritual responsibility, and commit to walking in the unshakeable order of your Creator!

Chapter 4

Let Him Be the Man

In His infinite wisdom, God established a divine order—a perfect plan for righteousness and responsibility that reverberates all the way from Genesis into eternity. This is not just ancient history. This is a living truth for us today, relevant for every man and woman, husband and wife, leader and servant in the body of Christ.

The Divine Order of Creation

Everything in the Word of God points us back to beginnings, back to foundations, because if the foundations are destroyed, what can the righteous do? (Psalm 11:3). If you want to understand why so many homes are in turmoil, why leadership is confused, why families are fractured, go back to the beginning—back to the garden, back to the Word.

The Bible focuses heavily on the God-given roles of men and women in marriage, and it all begins with the story of Adam and Eve. God did not leave the design of the marriage covenant to chance. He set His imprint in creation itself. "Therefore a man shall leave his father and mother and be joined to his wife, and they shall become one flesh" (Genesis 2:24 NKJV). Notice, this command was set long before

Adam and Eve ever had children—before there were fathers and mothers.

God was establishing the pattern for all future generations, telling us that the order of the household and of the planet would be rooted in unity, responsibility, and covenantal love.

The First Assignment: Vision Before Partnership

Let's pause and look deeper: God made the man first, forming him from the dust of the ground, breathing life into him—a unique action, not repeated with any other creature (Genesis 2:7). From the beginning, God was intentional—He gave man identity and vision before giving him partnership. He placed Adam in the garden, assigned him to work it and keep it, giving him both purpose and responsibility. This responsibility—this "keeping" of the garden—was not merely agricultural; it was spiritual, emotional, and moral. Adam was called to steward, to cover, to guard.

Only after He did all this did God say, "It is not good that man should be alone; I will make him a helper fit for him" (Genesis 2:18). God Himself recognized that Adam, alone, could not represent the fullness of God's relational image. Adam needed partnership, not just for procreation, but for purpose: "just right" for him, custom-designed—not an afterthought or an accessory, but a necessity to fulfill heaven's assignment on earth.

After God created the woman, Adam's very first words were a statement of revelation and unity: "This is now bone of my bones, and flesh of my flesh" (Genesis 2:23). He saw himself in his wife. He knew that hurting her would be hurting himself. This was not just sentiment but spiritual reality. The two become one flesh—living in transparency, vulnerability, love, and purpose. Marriage, in God's eyes, reflects Christ and His church, a model for godly unity that brings heaven to your home.

Yet, even with such a perfect beginning, what happened next exposes the subtlety of sin and the tragedy of abdication.

The Abdication of Responsibility

Genesis 3 is one of the most sobering chapters in all of Scripture. The serpent enters the picture—not as a colorful part of creation, but as the mouthpiece of rebellion, targeting God's design by attacking created order. The enemy did not go directly to Adam, the leader, but to the woman. Why? Because Satan knew Adam had the command, the Word, the covering—he was the one responsible to hold the line.

The serpent questions God's words, instigating doubt. "Did God actually say…?" (Genesis 3:1). Eve engages with him, but the Bible makes it clear—Adam was not far away. Genesis 3:6 says, "She also gave some to her husband who was with her, and he ate." The implication is harrowing: Adam was present, silent, passive. He did not intervene. He did not speak God's Word. He did not guard the garden. Be forewarned: to be present but absent is the undoing of leadership. To watch a spiritual attack unfold and say nothing is itself a great sin.

Paul drives this home in 1 Timothy 2:14: "Adam was not deceived, but the woman being deceived was in the transgression." Adam did not act out of ignorance; he rejected responsibility. He chose peace at any price, even at the price of truth and destiny. He abdicated his calling to cover, to protect, to "step up" at the very hour he was needed most.

The Cost of Man's Passivity

Let this resound for every Christian man, husband, and father: passivity was Adam's downfall, and if you let passivity set in, it will be yours too. Whether you are letting the culture, your workplace, or even your children dictate the atmosphere of your home instead of taking spiritual initiative, you have left your post. You have surrendered your spiritual authority and allowed chaos to enter the garden God gave you.

The consequences were immediate and severe. God did not blame Eve. He addressed Adam. "And to the man he said, 'Since you listened to your wife and ate from the tree whose fruit I commanded you not to eat, the ground is cursed because of you. All your life you will struggle to scratch a living from it" (Genesis 3:17 NLT). The curse on the ground did not originate with Eve, who was deceived, but with Adam, who sinned. The leadership mantle came with accountability; when Adam abdicated, creation suffered.

Guarding Your Garden: Spiritual Leadership and Accountability

Let's bring this right home: God has given every one of us a "garden." It's your mind, your heart, your thought life, your household, your calling. You are to keep and guard it—not just from weeds and pests and bad habits, but from anything that would seek to disrupt God's created order or challenge His Word in your life.

How do you guard your garden? You do what Adam did not do—you speak the Word, you refuse the enemy's narrative, and you act. 2 Corinthians 10:5 is not a suggestion but a command: "Casting down imaginations, and every high thing that exalteth itself against the knowledge of God, and bringing into captivity every thought to the obedience of Christ." If you're not leading your thought life with the authority of God's Word, someone—or something—else will. If you're not covering your home in prayer and obedience, the world will fill that gap with chaos.

Husbands and Wives Together: Operating in Divine Purpose

Husbands, step up! Your leadership is not about domination, it's about protection and provision—spiritually, emotionally, physically. It means setting boundaries, showing up, and loving sacrificially. It's not enough to bring home a paycheck—you are called to bring God's presence, His wisdom, His courage into your house. The atmosphere in your home will often mirror your spiritual presence. Are your wife and children flourishing under your covering, or are they exposed because you have withdrawn?

Wives, your support is not about weakness, but power. When you choose to honor your husband's leadership, you are not giving up your value—you are magnifying it. You hold the ability to breathe life, to encourage, to pray, to build up the man God placed in your home to lead. Even when you are more experienced in an area, your willingness to let him lead positions your family for blessing and alignment. Unity is not uniformity—it is operating in distinct roles for one divine purpose.

Let's take a lesson from God's response after the Fall: He made coverings for Adam and Eve, signifying grace, protection, and new beginnings—even after failure. He barred access to the tree of life, so they would not be forever trapped in a fallen state (Genesis 3:21-22). God still intervenes with mercy, but the consequences of abdicated leadership are real: every child born since then has been "born in sin and shapen in iniquity" (Psalm 51:5), and every family, every society, is marked by what was lost in Eden.

Lessons from Abdication: The Cost and the Call

Brothers, don't think abdication of leadership is just about your role at home—it's about destiny. God's order is structural—it determines how blessings flow. When Adam failed, the effect rippled through generations, down to us. Your level of responsibility will determine the quality of life, honor, and blessing that your descendants experience. God's commands are not optional. Genesis 3:17 does not read as encouragement: "Because you have hearkened unto the voice of your wife, and have eaten of the tree, of which I commanded thee, saying, Thou shalt not eat of it: cursed is the ground for thy sake." There was a consequence for getting out of order.

The principle remains: if you neglect your assignment—spiritually, financially, emotionally—the ground becomes hard. Progress is toilsome. Home life withers. This is not about male superiority—rather, it's about divine assignment and the accountability attached to it. Eve's vulnerability came not from her design but from a vacuum in Adam's leadership. And when any man vacates his responsibility—when he remains silent in the face of deception—he not only exposes his wife but undermines the blessings of his household.

Let's get real: Eve was deceived, but Adam was outright disobedient. The chain of command is spiritual; God speaks to the man, the man to his wife and family. Responsibility flows downward, while honor and trust flow upward. When a husband loves his wife as Christ loves the church (Ephesians 5:25), she flourishes, children thrive, and the home becomes a sanctuary of peace—an outpost of heaven on earth.

The Created Order and Godly Roles: Moving from Misalignment to Alignment

Understanding your position in God's created order is not just about the here and now—it's about preparing for eternity. "Christ in us, the hope of glory" (Colossians 1:27) is not passive; it's preparation for rulership in the kingdom to come. Align yourself with divine order today so that when God entrusts you with true riches—heavenly responsibility—He can do so with confidence.

Adam's failure was not just for a moment; it carried forward through every generation, resulting in homes where men struggle to lead, and women default to filling the gap. Modern culture may mock biblical roles, but the Word does not change. Paul instructs, "Wives, submit yourselves unto your own husbands, as unto the Lord… Husbands, love your wives, even as Christ also loved the church, and gave himself for it" (Ephesians 5:22,25). Righteousness is not only about present well-being, but about faithfully preparing for eternal stewardship.

Let me bring home another lesson: the way you govern your marriage and household is training for how you will rule in the world to come. Adam was made "the prototype"—the original vessel, given dominion and vision from his Creator. The woman was not made as an afterthought, but as an answer to the man's assignment—she validates, she consummates, she brings wholeness and fulfillment to God's vision.

"She shall be called Woman, because she was taken out of Man" (Genesis 2:23). Here, Adam gives the woman the highest designation in creation, affirming not just her value, but her purpose. A godly home is not held together by brute force or intellect, but by spiritual unity—one flesh, one mission, one vision.

But here's the counterpoint from Genesis 3:17—when the man listens to anyone above God or refuses to represent God's Word, the curse is not only personal; it's environmental. Men, the stakes could not be higher: If you won't "cover" your family, the world will "cover" them in everything but God.

Guarding Your Garden: Intentionality, Structure, and Spiritual Warfare

Your "garden" is not just a plot of land—it's a spiritual territory. Guarding it means intentionality about every influence, every word, every visitor, every thought, every form of entertainment. Adam let a foreign voice speak unchallenged in his home. Don't let culture, media, or even close relatives become the voice that shapes your family.

God established order—Adam, then Eve—not as a value statement on gender, but as a structural strategy for blessing. Man receives the vision; woman consummates it and brings it to life. She is "asah," made by the same power as Adam, but fitted for complementary assignment. Do not underestimate her power! Her willingness to submit and support does not make her lesser—it positions her to magnify God's design and multiply the fruit of the home.

Men, remember: spiritual leadership requires courage. You don't just reject passivity; you embrace sacrificial love. The standard is Christ—"who, being in very nature God, did not consider equality with God something to be used to his own advantage; rather, he made himself nothing…" (Philippians 2:6-7). When you serve your family with humility and strength, the foundation is firm. When you abdicate, the ground is cursed.

Sisters, your role is no less spiritual. When you encourage, pray, and lend your strength to your husband's leadership, you are practicing kingdom dynamics. You are releasing order into chaos, blessing into confusion, life into dry places.

Redemption and the New Woman: From Eve to Mary

Thank God the story doesn't end in the garden. While Eve represents the vulnerability and failure in the natural, Mary represents the possibility and redemptive victory in the spiritual. Where Eve was deceived and Adam abdicated, Mary believed and brought forth the Savior. She is the "new woman"—her submission paved the way for Christ to enter and restore order to a broken world. Through Christ, the curse is not the final word—redemption breaks the cycle and sets the template for restored roles and refreshed blessing.

As you look at your own family, recognize that every moment of spiritual initiative, every courageous decision to "guard your garden," and every act of godly alignment is not just shaping your own household—it is shaping generations. You are writing your family's spiritual legacy.

Practical Applications: Stepping Up, Standing Strong

So what does this mean in everyday life?

Men, Step Up to Lead—Men, take the initiative in prayer, in decision-making, in the spiritual direction of your home. Admit when you're wrong, ask for forgiveness, and set the standard for humility and responsibility.

Women, Encourage and Empower—Women, actively support your husband's spiritual growth. Speak life into his calling, defer to his leadership in conflicting moments, trusting Christ who works in both of you. Your encouragement is a powerhouse. Your faith can steady him when he falters.

Both Parents, Train Up Children for Independence and Purpose. Prepare your children for adulthood not by doing everything for them, but by teaching them to hear from God, to wrestle with Scripture, to develop their own discipline and accountability. Help your sons to be leaders, your daughters to be courageous supporters and initiators for God's purpose.

Guard Your Personal Garden. Your thought life is the battleground. Cast down imaginations that challenge the knowledge of Christ. Guard what you consume, what you listen to, and what you speak. If it doesn't line up with the Word, throw it out.

Align With God's Commands, Not the World's Recommendations. God's Word is not open to reinterpretation by popular opinion. We live by His decrees, which are binding and non-negotiable. Don't weaken your home's foundation by mixing truth with the world's philosophies.

Acknowledge the Cost of Abdication. Know that every time you fail to step into your role, something precious is compromised—not just in the present, but for the future. Adam's silence was the doorway for the enemy; your silence is his invitation.

Embrace Grace and New Beginnings. If you have failed, take it to the cross, receive forgiveness, and start again. God covered Adam and Eve, but He also redirected their future.

Legacy: Filling the Heavenlies

Finally, never forget—this life is not just about managing crises; it's about training for the next. Everything you do now—every stand you take for divine order, every refusal to abdicate, every choice to step up or support—is rehearsal for eternity. You are learning kingdom leadership, preparing for "good works which God prepared in advance for us to do" (Ephesians 2:10).

Paul writes, "If any man be in Christ, he is a new creature" (2 Corinthians 5:17). If there was failure in the garden, there is victory in the cross. If Adam's legacy was abdication, your legacy in Christ is spiritual courage, order, and blessing that can turn families, cities, and nations back to their Creator.

Let him be the man God called him to be; let her be the "just-right" complement that magnifies the vision, and together you will see heaven's order and blessing fill your home.

The Mandate of the Garden

God formed the man from the dust of the ground. He breathed into Adam's nostrils the breath of life, and the man became a living being—animated by the very Spirit of God, set apart from every other creature by the intentionality of his Creator (Genesis 2:7). It was not an accident that God made man first and alone, placing him in the garden before there was a partner, before there was a family, before there was even a problem to solve. God set the divine order from the start.

Scripture tells us that after forming Adam, God placed him squarely in the garden of Eden, surrounded by abundance, beauty, and the undiluted presence of the Lord. But with that placement came an assignment: "The LORD God placed the man in the Garden of Eden to tend and watch over it" (Genesis 2:15 NLT). There is no ambiguity in God's command here—the man was not just a passive recipient of paradise, but the steward and protector of God's creation. His charge was to watch over, to cultivate, to guard, and to keep order. That charge was practical—working the soil—but it was even more so spiritual and moral: Adam was to set the tone for all of creation.

God's wisdom in this is extraordinary. He did not give Adam a partner first—He gave him vision, responsibility, and purpose. God's blueprint for healthy relationships and strong families always begins with vision before partnership. As men, you receive the assignment, the "Word from the Lord" about your garden—your family, your marriage, your calling—before God brings someone to partner with you in that work. That vision cannot be skipped, replaced, or outsourced. Husbands, fathers, single men: your first calling is always to walk in God's presence, to listen, to obey, and to set the environment for everything that follows.

The Purpose of the Union of Man and Woman

Yet, after all this, it was God—not Adam—who recognized a limitation. There was no suitable helper for him on earth. Notice the heart of the Creator: Adam did not even recognize his need but God addressed it. The "helper" is not an afterthought or a subordinate, but a complement—someone who fills in what is lacking, who brings out the fullness of God's image in relationship and unity.

This is not just about companionship or alleviating loneliness—it is about fulfilling purpose. Man alone could not fully reflect the relational, creative, and governing heart of God. The woman would step in to help him fulfill his assignment—not only as a support, but as an essential part of realizing the fullness of heaven's design. Her presence does not diminish the man's leadership but awakens it; her partnership does not erase his responsibility but magnifies it.

When God brought the woman to Adam, a miracle of recognition took place. Adam awoke from his deep sleep and met the one who was both like him and yet breathtakingly unique: "This is now bone of my bones, and flesh of my flesh; she shall be called Woman, for she was taken out of Man" (Genesis 2:23). Adam saw himself in her; he saw destiny, unity, reflection—God's handiwork up close. This was more than romance; it was revelation and assignment. Adam was, in essence, declaring: "If I injure you, I injure myself. If I bless you, I bless myself. God has created us for each other, with each other, to fulfill this divine purpose as one in Him."

What happened next, however, forever changed the trajectory of humanity. It is not just a cautionary tale for Adam and Eve; it is a prophetic warning for every husband, father, and leader across all generations.

The Tragedy of Silence

Adam did not falter because he was out working in the garden while Eve was left on her own. He was right there: silent, watching, disengaged while a spiritual crisis unfolded before his eyes. Genesis 3:6 records, "She also gave some [fruit] to her husband, who was with her, and he ate it." This is the abdication of biblical manhood: to be present in body but absent in responsibility; to be a silent witness while chaos enters the garden you are called to keep. While the serpent spun his web of deception, Adam failed to speak the truth of God, failed to challenge the invader, and failed to protect the one he was designed to cover.

Paul's insight in 1 Timothy 2:14 exposes the issue all the more: "Adam was not deceived, but the woman being deceived was in the transgression." Eve was led astray—but Adam, who knew better, chose not to act. This is not mere weakness, but outright irresponsibility. God's judgment echoes down to us in Genesis 3:17: "Because you have listened to the voice of your wife and have eaten from the tree about which I commanded you, saying, 'You must not eat from it,' cursed is the ground because of you." Adam listened to the wrong voice. He was designed to be the leader and spiritual head, but he relinquished the post—and as a result, the ground, the environment, the blessing, became cursed.

Let me bring this home to you. Blessing and order flow through the structures that God creates. When men step out of alignment, when they become passive or relinquish responsibility, a vacuum is created and disorder rushes in to fill it. Adam's silence was not just a private sin—it had cosmic consequences. His passivity allowed the serpent to redefine and reframe God's original design, and it is the same for men today. When you refuse to step up, your marriage, your children, and even your community suffer loss.

Leadership in God's kingdom is not about dominating others but about "keeping" the garden—maintaining the right spiritual atmosphere, advancing God's agenda, loving sacrificially, and speaking truth even when it becomes uncomfortable. It is about doing what Adam did not: naming, affirming, covering, standing up and saying, "As for me and my house, we will serve the Lord" (Joshua 24:15).

To the men, I say—this is not about being perfect, but about being present, intentional, and surrendered to your divine assignment. You are called to be the "head gardener," responsible before God. Even if you do not feel adequate, His appointment is your empowerment. Begin by setting the spiritual temperature—pray with your wife, speak the Scriptures over your family, admit wrong, correct course, show humility, and reject every voice that is not from the throne.

Women, your strength does not compete with your husband's calling, it completes it. Your willingness to support his leadership is not weakness but wisdom. By encouraging, praying, and speaking life into your man, you are empowering him to step into the fullness of his calling.

Living By the Principles of the Created Order

Consider this truth: in family life, the "created order" and the weight of accountability are not abstract doctrines, but the living principles that protect your home from chaos and compromise. Adam's charge to "keep the garden" is a model for every role in the household. Your mind, your marriage, the culture you cultivate at the dinner table, even the spiritual atmosphere of heaven in your parenting—that's your "garden." Guard it. Don't let the enemy, in whatever form, walk in and rewrite the vision God has given you.

True leadership can be challenging. Sometimes, the garden is peaceful, and sometimes it is beset by storms—small disputes, financial stress, temptations of distraction, or outright attacks on unity. Modern culture often scoffs at biblical roles. The world says, "Do what feels right for you. There's no difference between men and women, husband and wife—all roles are interchangeable, leadership is unnecessary." But God's Word is the final authority, not societal trends.

I remind you that your "garden" is not just your household but your thought life, your principles, and your heart's orientation. Just as Adam was charged with casting out what did not belong, so you too must cast down imaginations that rise up against the knowledge of God (2 Corinthians 10:5).

Be vigilant: are there voices—media, old habits, negative confessions—that you have allowed in? Are there places in your marriage or in your mind where you have surrendered ground to the enemy? Repent, take authority, reclaim what God entrusted to you. Don't wait for someone else to do it.

The Cost of Maintaining Boundaries

Guarding your garden will cost you. It requires sacrifice and steadfastness. Sometimes it means confronting uncomfortable issues, asking for forgiveness, refusing to let bitterness take root or the sun go down on your anger, and choosing to love unconditionally. At times, guarding your garden means being misunderstood, criticized, or challenged by those who do not comprehend the divine order. Stand firm; the order of God is under attack in every generation.

Remember, the created order comes with divine boundaries and supernatural potential with eternal consequences. God gave Adam command over the planet—he was not only to keep his own life in order but also to establish the culture of the human race. The woman was to validate, consummate, and multiply the impact of the man's obedience. When that alignment was broken, disorder entered. The fall of Adam was the fall of mankind—but in Christ, the Last Adam, we see the power of restored roles and reset blessings.

Misalignment is costly, but godly roles restore what was lost. I challenge you not to treat God's Word as a set of recommendations but as commands to be lived. There is no room for half-heartedness, no margin for spiritual laziness: Adam's abdication of leadership brought a curse, but Jesus' assumption of responsibility brought redemption and blessing. Now, as men and women of God, we are called to build a culture of righteousness into our homes—a foretaste of the kingdom to come.

Godly Leadership Is Not About Your Way

Godly leadership is not about getting your way; it's about aligning with Christ, who "loved the church and gave himself up for her" (Ephesians 5:25). To love sacrificially is to lead spiritually, and to lead spiritually is to serve with humility, vision, and courage.

Ladies, your leadership role is no less critical—your affirmation, encouragement, and trust empower your husband's calling and speak peace and order into the home for the benefit of your children. When both roles align, heaven's blessing meets your household in tangible ways.

What does this look like in practice?

It means husbands making decisions, not for their comfort, but for the good of the entire family—sometimes saying "no" to things that would seem good but would bring disorder or compromise. It means listening, serving, and repenting quickly. It means wives trusting the Lord enough to allow their husbands to lead, even when it takes faith and prayer. It means refusing to allow the enemy to set your home's agenda.

It means children receiving training their parents about how to function in godly roles in life. Don't carry your children emotionally or spiritually forever—raise sons who will lead, daughters who will partner with God and with the men to whom God assigns them. Give your children the gifts of love, discipline, faith in Christ, and accountability. If you do, you prepare them not only for earthly responsibility, but for kingdom collaboration in eternity.

Never assume that your marriage, your family, your "garden," will take care of itself. Guarding what God has entrusted you with is active, ongoing, and strategic. Genesis 3 shows us the cost of neglect. Don't let silence be your legacy; let it be courageous leadership.

God's framework does not diminish women but empowers them to be destiny-shapers and legacy-makers. Remember, the woman was made by the same creative power as Adam, not less, but distinct. When she validates and encourages, she breathes supernatural life into the family vision. Together, their unity empowers heaven's reign on earth.

Coming Full Circle in Christ

Let's come full circle in Christ. The curse is broken and a new pattern is set. Where Adam failed, Jesus succeeded.

Through Mary, the "new woman," the Savior entered the world and restored the possibility for every home to walk in redeemed order. Each act of spiritual leadership, sacrificial love, affirmation, and unity is a participation in God's redemptive work.

Let's reclaim our roles, align with God's purpose, and transform our families and futures by honoring the structure God set from the beginning. This is how we "guard our garden," build our legacy, and prepare for eternity's reward.

Questions for Meditation

1. Where in my own life, marriage, or thought life have I chosen the comfort of silence and passivity instead of actively standing up for God's truth?

2. What specific worldly influences, media, or unchecked thoughts have I allowed into my spiritual garden, and how can I cast them out today using the authority of 2 Corinthians 10:5?

3. For Men: Am I actively covering my wife and children in prayer, leading them with sacrificial love, or have I withdrawn and left my family spiritually exposed?

4. For Women: How can I more intentionally use my God-given strength to validate, encourage, and speak life into my husband's leadership to bring our home into divine alignment?

5. How do my daily choices, boundaries, and reactions within my household reflect the order of heaven and prepare my family for our eternal destiny in Christ?

Call to Action

The time for passivity is over. God has called you to guard your garden, honor His created order, and build a spiritual legacy that will echo through generations.

Men, step up to lead your home with sacrificial love and unwavering courage. Reject the silence of the first Adam and embrace the redemptive power of Jesus Christ. Cover your family in prayer, set holy boundaries, and stand firm against the whispers of the enemy.

Women, rise up in your divine strength and purpose. Empower your husband's calling with your faith, your support, and your steadfast prayers.

Together, reclaim your God-given roles and align your household with the blueprint of heaven. Do not leave your family's future to chance or allow the culture to dictate your values. Take spiritual responsibility today, secure your legacy, and watch the Lord transform your home into a powerful sanctuary of His grace!

Chapter 5

The Abandonment of Created Order

The woman was created to be a powerful complement to the man. She was designed to validate and help fulfill the vision God had already given him. She was the "just-right" woman. Adam looked at her and said, "This is now bone of my bones, and flesh of my flesh." He affirmed God's miraculous work. But what happened next reveals the tragedy of man's abdication of his God-appointed role.

The Serpent Approached the Woman

Everything changed when the serpent entered the garden. Genesis 3 details the breakdown of the roles God established. The serpent approached the woman and began to question the commands of God. He said, "Did God really say you must not eat the fruit from any of the trees in the garden?" We have just considered a crucial question in the last chapter: Where was Adam while the devil was talking to his wife?

Genesis 3:6 gives us the chilling answer. When the woman saw that the fruit of the tree was good for food and pleasing to the eye, she took some and ate it. She also gave some to her husband, *who was with her*, and he ate it.

Adam Was Right There

Adam was right there. He allowed a beast of the field—a creature he had personally named and been given dominion over—to cross-examine his wife and challenge the Creator.

The Apostle Paul says in 1 Timothy 2:14: *"And Adam was not deceived, but the woman being deceived was in the transgression."* Adam knew exactly what God had said. He had received the command directly from the mouth of God before the woman was even created. Adam was not tricked; he was irresponsible. He abdicated his responsibility to lead and protect his wife. He should have stepped in front of Eve, looked at that serpent, and commanded it to leave the garden. He should have shut down the noise of the enemy right then and there. But he stood by silently. He failed to intervene. He failed to speak God's Word. He failed to guard the garden God gave him.

Because Adam relinquished his leadership and failed to cover his wife, the divine order was broken. When God came down to the garden to address the sin, He did not call out for the woman. He called out for the man, the priority of the created order. And in Genesis 3:17, God issues the penalty: *"Because you listened to your wife and ate fruit from the tree about which I commanded you, 'You must not eat from it,' Cursed is the ground because of you."*

The ground was cursed because of Adam's failure, not the woman's. The penalty fell on the man because he was the prototype. He was the one responsible for the planet. He allowed his home to fall out of alignment with heaven.

Men Must Actively Defend Their Territory

God left it up to the first man to take care of business in the Garden of Eden, and He is leaving it up to you to take care of business in your garden today.

Men, what is your garden? Let's get practical and personal—your garden is the sum of all that God has entrusted to you: your thought life, your heart, your values, your principles, and the atmosphere within your home. It's your marriage, your family, your inner world, and even the legacy you are building for the next generation.

Adam's garden was Eden, but your "garden" is wherever God has positioned you to cultivate, keep, and defend heaven's priorities. God expects you to actively defend your territory. He expects you to take care of business not just by biding your time, but by actively tending, weeding, and protecting the territory God has assigned to you.

Guarding your garden means you must stand watch against distractions, lies, and every external influence that threatens God's order in your life and home. In the garden, Adam's failure was not only inaction—it was inattention. He allowed a foreign voice to enter unquestioned, unchecked, unchallenged.

The enemy still whispers into homes, marriages, minds, and ministries today, eager to sow confusion, cultivate doubt, and replace heaven's culture with chaos. That serpent might wear the face of worldly culture, pop psychology, bitterness from past wounds, lazy parenting, or unresolved conflicts. It might come as pride, fear, busyness—even "practical wisdom" that isn't rooted in Scripture.

You guard your garden by first watching over your inner life. Sow the Word daily into your mind and heart; water it with prayer and worship. Pull out the weeds of resentment, neglect, and spiritual apathy before they take root. If you sense a thought or influence that doesn't align with God's truth, don't negotiate—evict it. Bring every imagination, every fantasy, every fear, every rogue opinion captive to Christ (2 Corinthians 10:5).

Don't let worldly philosophies or external circumstances tell you how to think or how to lead—it's your responsibility before God to guard what's been entrusted to you, just as Adam was commanded to "dress and keep the garden" (Genesis 2:15). You are not a spiritual tourist; you are the appointed keeper of Eden's borders in your world.

Get Engaged in the Leadership of Your Family

Let's make this even more concrete. For many, the "garden" also includes the relational and spiritual climate of your marriage.

Husbands the charge is for you to be present—not simply there in body but engaged in spirit. It's about taking initiative to protect your wife, bless her, lead her in prayer, and drive out anything that would undermine her sense of security and purpose. Adam's silence in the face of the serpent's lies was not mere passivity; it was abdication. Don't leave the door open for deception to enter your home! Speak up, set standards, protect your household by covering your wife and children in prayer, with Scripture, and in loving correction when needed.

Wives, your "garden" encompasses your heart attitude, your support, the words of your mouth, and your partnership in the Spirit. You have a unique anointing to nurture faith, encourage vision, and help hold the family's course steady whenever the winds shift.

Women, you are kingmakers. The role of helpmeet (Genesis 2:18) means more than just an assistant. It means to come alongside as a strong and essential spiritual partner who completes the family leadership. Your encouragement reinvigorates a husband who feels the weight of leadership; your prayers can strengthen his backbone to stand when spiritual warfare intensifies. It is not weakness to submit and honor your husband's God-given leadership—it is strength under control, faith in action, and trust in God's order.

Husbands, guarding your garden means recognizing the cost of neglect. When you leave the territory of your mind unchecked, resentment, self-pity, bitterness or fear can run wild. When you watch silently while conversation in your home shifts into dishonor, you are guilty of allowing weeds to choke out blessings. The moment you, as a husband, refuse to address an ongoing bitterness or ignore your responsibility to discipline with love, you "step aside" like Adam—inviting the enemy to fill the gap. The moment you, as a wife, become a chronic critic, withhold respect, or undermine your husband's efforts, you participate in disorder—the ground of your home grows harder, harmony becomes rare, blessing is hindered.

Set Boundaries in the Spirit

Take to heart what I teach you. The created order means you are individually and mutually responsible to "cast down imaginations and every lofty thing that exalts itself against the knowledge of God" (2 Corinthians 10:5). That applies to your mind and your family. There are spiritual boundaries to enforce—and it begins with the discipline to reject anything that tries to occupy territory meant for God's truth.

Parents, raise your children to recognize and reject unrighteous influences. Be unapologetically alert and intentional about the media that plays in your house and your child's phone, the books your family reads, the attitudes tolerated at the dinner table, and the environment you foster to shape identity. What you normalize, you multiply.

Your garden is also the garden of your choices—the power, as Adam had, to choose obedience or abdication. God did not remove Adam's ability to choose, even though He knew what was coming. God's order is never lost, only transferred. If you refuse to act, the enemy will jump in. If you step out of godly order, something else will fill the vacuum, and it usually isn't godly.

None of us has a perfect garden. Each of us, whether husband or wife, parent or child, faces daily tests where the enemy tries to inject the lust of the flesh, the lust of the eyes, and the pride of life. Your key to resisting these temptations is vigilance—intentional, loving, scripturally grounded leadership in your sphere. Even Adam and Eve, after their failure, experienced God's covering. He made garments for them from animal skins, showing mercy and introducing a new eternal order that would come through the blood of Jesus to cover our sins. He banned them from the tree of life so that their fallen state wouldn't become eternal.

Be Vigilant

Men, your family will flourish when you put Christ at the center, stand on God's promises, and drive out every serpent that sneaks in through entertainment, conversation or your neglect. Own up to your mistakes. Apologize when you fail. Set boundaries and hold to them, even when it's hard. Gather your wife and children in prayer. Lead them into God's presence at home and take them to church.

Women, reinforce your husband's leadership with faith-filled prayers and affirming words—even when he struggles. Be the first to cast down thoughts of competition, self-pity, or exasperation, and replace them with intercession and encouragement. The "garden" flourishes where the helpmeet waters it with honor, patience, affirmation, and godly expectations. Don't let cultural lies against submission drain the joy from your relationship. Embrace the power of the Holy Spirit that made you one. Tend your garden today, and generations will rise up to bless you tomorrow!

What happened in Genesis 3 is not an isolated event, but an ongoing demonic strategy—an attack against God's structure in your family, your marriage, and even in how you see yourself. The devil targets the headship of men and the unity with their wives because he knows once divine order is broken, God's Spirit is hindered.

Disagree with Anything That Contradicts God

Recall the scene—Adam stood present as the serpent deceived Eve, yet his silence gave the enemy access. He failed to speak truth, leaving room for lies to take root in the heart of his wife. Today's "serpents" may not look like talking animals, but the sound of their voices penetrates clearly through news, social media, entertainment, gossip, cultural pressures, and our own unchecked thoughts. Their power lies not just in what is said, but in our failure to contradict what is said by God's Word.

Second Corinthians 10:5 is not just a verse to memorize. It is a strategy for private victory: "Casting down imaginations, and every high thing that exalts itself against the knowledge of God, and bringing into captivity every thought to the obedience of Christ."

Imaginations are ideas, mental pictures, and narratives—some inspired by the Lord, others by the enemy. "High things" include prideful attitudes or cultural standards that challenge God's wisdom for the family and world. God hates a high look. He loves humility.

Taking thoughts captive is not passive; it is decisive spiritual combat. Examine every thought: Does it align with the Word? Does this seem like Christ's command? If not, bind it, cast it down, and refuse to give it a foothold.

Maintaining a garden free of spiritual weeds is the difference between chaos and peace, between desert and oasis. What voices have you allowed in without challenge? Music, media, lotteries, friends, and traditions can all whisper things contrary to God's truth.

Keep Your Family Covered

Husbands and fathers, your calling is not just to oversee or direct—but to cover. Be the spiritual leader. When a crisis happens, be the first to pray, to repent, to correct what's out of order. You may not always have the answers, but you can always demonstrate that you know you should turn to God.

Wives, your call to support and nurture is no less spiritual. By honoring, encouraging, and praying under your husband's leadership when he's home and boldly when you're alone with your children, you build a wall of strength around your home. If you see danger first or have greater experience in an area, your prayers and affirmation empower him to lead more courageously. Choosing to "stand down" so he can step up is a spiritual discipline that invites order and grace into your marriage and strength into your children. Your support is prophetic—it shapes generations.

Women, embrace your authority as a helper. You are anointed to wage war in prayer, discern danger through spirituality, encourage with wisdom, and help hold the course in turbulent seasons. As Eve was deceived when Adam went silent, homes can be left unprotected if voices of truth and affirmation are absent. Your words, worship, and wisdom form a faith-reservoir from which your husband and children draw strength.

Be a Blessing to Families and Nations

God's created order is not a suggestion. It is the foundation of life and godliness, not only for individuals but for nations.

"If you fully obey the LORD your God and carefully keep all his commands that I am giving you today, the LORD your God will set you high above all the nations of the world. You will experience all these blessings if you obey the LORD your God" (Deuteronomy 28:1-2 NLT).

When Adam sinned against God, the ground was cursed. When men reject their role of spiritual leadership under God, families and societies experience drought and disorder.

God's call is not merely to resist evil, but to cultivate good. When you embrace your God-given role as a husband or a wife, you create an environment of blessing in your house.

Misalignment opens the door for generational disorder. If you tolerate disunity, disrespect, or mediocrity, your children learn to treat God and God's order as a distant and disgraced option. But when your children see you tending the garden, pulling out weeds of pride, confessing your faults to one another, forgiving and serving one another, and living by the Word, they learn to cherish and guard God's garden themselves. You are setting a pattern not just for today, but for generations to follow. Nations will be influenced by your family's spirit until the Lord returns.

Create consecration boundaries around phone and TV screens, friendships, conversations, finances, and time together as a family. Create an environment where Christ is honored, the Spirit is welcomed, and every serpent is named and expelled. Let the fruit in your garden be the fruit of the Spirit—love, joy, peace, patience, kindness, goodness, faithfulness, gentleness, and self-control (Galatians 5:22-23).

Discern the Battles

Sometimes the serpent whispers through friends, "Let the kids decide for themselves," or, "It's not worth the fight," or, "Everyone else does it this way." Sometimes the most dangerous weeds are apathy, compromise, and weary silence. Rise up, Man of God. Take your stand, Woman of God. Put on the whole armor of God. Get your spiritual gardening tools ready, and do not rest until your garden grows and displays the beauty and order that God intended.

And in all this, let us never forget—outside Christ there is no hope of true and lasting order or redemption. Adam failed, but the Last Adam—Jesus Christ—never did! Through Christ, the curse is not the final word. You have spiritual weapons. You have authority in Jesus' name. You have the indwelling Holy Spirit. You are not powerless before the serpent, but triumphant through the blood of Christ and the promises of God's Word.

Guard your garden with diligence. Cover your home with prayer. Maintain the unity of the Spirit in the bond of peace. Refuse to surrender territory to the lies of the enemy. When you see disorder, step up and take action—call on heaven's resources, wield the sword of the Spirit, and keep your place at the gate. You are not just fighting for your peace, but for your legacy, your children, and for kingdom impact in the age to come.

Take Your Thoughts Captive to Truth

Don't let Satan lead you or counsel you! Every time you entertain thoughts that contradict God's Word about your identity, marriage, or authority, you grant the enemy a foothold. Adam stood by while an unsanctioned voice whispered suspicion against his God into the garden God had given him to guard. The serpent didn't overpower Eve. He just talked longer and invited her to doubt God's order until she convinced her husband to take an overt act of rebellion.

If a thought or imagination challenges what God says about your calling as a spouse or parent, cast it down and drive it out of your life. We "cast down imaginations, and every high thing that exalts itself against the knowledge of God." Do not negotiate. Arrest it, interrogate it with Scripture, and expel it. Refuse to let your mind or family be a playground for the enemy's lies. Mark every lie "Return to Sender" by declaring God's truth over your situation.

Persevere

Driving out the wrong voices is not a one-time act, but a lifelong discipline. The enemy persistently adapts his tactics. Sometimes he sneaks in through stress, busyness, or advice that feels 'wise' but is out of sync with the heart of God. There is no substitute for ongoing, Spirit-led vigilance: daily time in the Word, daily prayers for your spouse and children, and daily encouragement between husband and wife.

When spiritual attack comes—when disharmony, cynicism, or apathy overtake gratitude and faith—stand strong in the Lord. Don't cede authority by silence or resignation. Adam's abdication brought a curse not only to himself but to generations after him. But your decision now—to speak faith, to course correct, to lead humbly—can set a blessing in motion for generations to come.

God's Word is not a set of suggestions; these are divine commands, establishing the atmosphere for growth and legacy. You must return every false thought—every "high thing" that exalts itself above the knowledge of God—by declaring, "This is not what my Father says about me or my family!" This is how you enforce spiritual boundaries. You do not stand alone; you stand with the authority of the Word, with the backing of heaven, and in the victory secured by Jesus.

Stand Firm in Christ

Standing strong in the Lord is not an option; it is your calling. Step forward and reclaim every area the enemy has tried to occupy. Husbands, protect your wife not just physically, but emotionally and spiritually. Lead in prayer, encouragement, and repentance. Wives, use your prayers and affirmation to empower and uplift your husband. Set the spiritual climate that makes home like heaven.

Your vigilance as parents teaches your children not just with words, but by example. They'll see if resentment or distraction is tolerated, and they'll see when prayer, confession, and resilience are practiced. Be intentional: plant truth, water it with worship and encouragement, prune distractions, and confront anything that snatches away God's Word. Double guard vulnerable places with prayer, accountability, and spiritual disciplines.

To stand strong in the Lord is daily surrender to God's way. You wield spiritual authority through humility, confrontation of disorder, and reliance on God's intended partnership between husband and wife. When you walk as one in action and purpose, the combined power pushes back the darkness and establishes godly order.

Make Jesus Your Ultimate Example

Remember, Christ is the true example. Where Adam was silent, Jesus is the Word made flesh. Where Adam abdicated, Jesus took full responsibility. Where the first marriage failed, the new covenant is restored—made possible and powerful in Him. Bring every thought captive to Christ, and take your place as guardian of the garden entrusted to you.

You stand strong not by might, but by faith in God and the power of the Holy Spirit. Assume your post. Watch, pray, and act. Having done all, stand firm!

Live Out Godly Roles

Men, authentic leadership means taking responsibility for the spiritual and emotional health of your home. Protect and support your wife and children, ensuring their sense of value and security. Failing to act—by ignoring conflict, refusing to set boundaries, or lacking godly example—creates a spiritual vacuum that breeds disorder.

Restore and Maintain Biblical Alignment

We must move from misalignment back to godly assignment. God's Word is filled with commands, not mere suggestions. God calls us to holy living, with clear roles and responsibilities.

Ephesians 5:25 instructs, "Husbands, love your wives, even as Christ also loved the church, and gave himself for it." Men, your love must be sacrificial and courageous, covering and protecting your wife. Without this, you are out of God's order. Wives, your charge is equally powerful—encourage, support, and help your husband step into his God-given leadership. Even when you have answers or feel more capable in an area, empower him to lead so your home flourishes in alignment with heaven.

Righteousness is not just about present harmony, but preparation for eternal responsibilities. The way you lead your home now is training for kingdom roles in the world to come.

Through the redemptive work of Jesus—the Last Adam—we have power to restore what the first Adam lost. Christ in us is the answer for misalignment and disorder. Embrace your role. Keep God's order. If you tend your garden, God will send His blessing down on your home.

Questions for Meditation

1. In what areas of my life have I "stepped aside" when God was calling me to step up and take responsibility?

2. Men. How does recognizing that Adam was an irresponsible sinner, rather than deceived, change my view of taking spiritual leadership in the home?

3. What ungodly thoughts or "imaginations" must I cast down to properly guard the garden of my mind and my family?

4. Men: Am I loving my wife with Christ's sacrificial, protective love, or passively allowing the enemy to speak into her life?

5. Women: How can I better encourage and validate my husband's spiritual leadership to bring our home into biblical alignment?

Call to Action

Men, rise up! Take responsibility for the spiritual atmosphere in your home. Don't remain silent when challenges arise. Guard your garden with God's Word.

Women, support and encourage your husband's leadership. Resist the urge to take control; instead, empower him to be the man God created him to be, so together you can bring your family into biblical order and experience heaven's blessing.

Chapter 6
From Eve to Mary: God's Design for Redemption

We are stepping into a profound revelation about the dual inheritance that every believer carries. You must understand the magnitude of what God has done from the beginning of time all the way through the cross. We are looking at the legacy of two mothers—the legacy of creation and the legacy of redemption.

When you look at the Scriptures, you see a master plan unfolding. Eve, the first woman, was created to bear the children of the earth. She was the mother of all living. But Mary, the redemptive woman, was chosen by Almighty God to bear the Son who would populate the heavens!

If you are a born-again believer, you inherit both incredible legacies. Physically, naturally, you carry the lineage of Eve. But spiritually, you carry the legacy of Mary—a divine capacity to yield to the Holy Spirit, to be overshadowed by the power of the Most High, and to birth something eternal into your generation. You are not just living for yourself. You are not just trying to survive your circumstances. You are in eternity training right now. God placed a competency inside of you to nurture life that impacts both earth and heaven, and it is time for you to walk in that authority.

God's Design for Marriage: Mr. and Mrs. Adam

To understand the redemptive glory of Mary, we first have to look back at the original perfection of the first woman. Before the Fall, before sin corrupted the earth, there was a flawless, divine structure.

Look at Genesis 5:1-2:
"In the day that God created man, in the likeness of God made he him; Male and female created he them; and blessed them, and called their name Adam, in the day when they were created."

God called *their* name Adam! They shared a corporate identity. They shared a unified vision. When I stand with my wife, people do not see two completely separate, disjointed individuals running in opposite directions. They see Mr. and Mrs. Wellington Boone. We operate under one name, one covenant, and one mandate. That is a throwback to the original created order. Before she was ever called Eve, she was Mrs. Adam!

When God said in Genesis 2:18, *"It is not good that the man should be alone; I will make him an help meet for him,"* He was not just talking about giving Adam a companion so he wouldn't be lonely. He was establishing the foundational family structure for the entire planet. Adam was a seed man. God was structuring the family so that out of their union, the earth would be populated with children who reflected the glory of the Creator. God was not just looking for population; He was looking for destination.

Both Adam and his wife were physically and spiritually perfect. Think about it. When Adam looked at her and said, *"This is now bone of my bones, and flesh of my flesh,"* he was looking at the masterful, unblemished handiwork of God. She had no flaws. She had no bumps, no spots, no sickness, no insecurity. God used the same divine power—the Hebrew concept of *ASAH*, meaning to make or create with divine intentionality—to form her that He used to form the man. She was beautiful and she was brought to Adam by the Creator Himself.

But we know what happened. Adam abdicated his responsibility. He stepped aside when he should have stepped up, and sin entered the bloodline. Because of that catastrophic failure, Eve became the mother of all living *sinners*. The seed of sin was passed down generationally. The children of the earth were born into a fallen state, shaped in iniquity.

The first family brought children to live in the physical earth, but those children were broken. Humanity could not fix its own state of being. We needed a Redeemer. We needed a Last Adam. And to bring the Last Adam into the world, God chose a new kind of woman.

The Redemptive Woman: A Standard of Greatness

Thousands of years after the garden, an angel named Gabriel steps into the timeline of human history. Gabriel is a powerful messenger of God. He appeared to the prophet Daniel in the Old Testament, and now he appears to a young virgin in Nazareth.

Read the words of Gabriel carefully in Luke 1:30-32:
"And the angel said unto her, Fear not, Mary: for thou hast found favor with God. And, behold, thou shalt conceive in thy womb, and bring forth a son, and shalt call his name

Jesus. He shall be great, and shall be called the Son of the Highest."

The angel Gabriel did not appear to Mary by accident. God does not throw His eternal plans at random targets. Mary met a high, rigorous spiritual standard that allowed her to carry greatness in her womb. She was a virgin, yes, but her purity was not just physical; her purity was profoundly spiritual.

Mary asks the angel a very practical question in verse 34: *"How shall this be, seeing I know not a man?"*

There is no shame in her voice. There is a quiet confidence. She is espoused to Joseph, but she has kept herself pure. She protected her vessel. In today's culture, people mock purity. The world laughs at holiness. But heaven honors it! Mary's virginity was a testament to her character. She lived a life completely set apart for God.

God sending the angel Gabriel tells you everything you need to know about the standard of being she was. She qualified to bear greatness in her womb.

Women, listen to me right now. When you look at your children, or when you look at your own potential, you must never dismiss it as ordinary. Sometimes a child is full of energy, or maybe they struggle in a school system built for conformity, and people are quick to label them as "slow" or "problematic." Do not ever speak that over your seed! You did not carry "stupid." You did not carry "average." You carry greatness! Spiritually, your lineage as a believer is defined by the favor found in Mary. You are carrying eternal potential.

Everything Gabriel spoke over Mary was purely redemptive. It was designed to fix what broke in the garden. When the serpent spoke to Eve, he released a spiritual poison that brought death. But when the angel spoke to Mary, he released a spiritual prophetic word that brought eternal life.

Overshadowed by the Holy Ghost

Look at the extraordinary promise in Luke 1:35:
"And the angel answered and said unto her, The Holy Ghost shall come upon thee, and the power of the Highest shall overshadow thee: therefore also that holy thing which shall be born of thee shall be called the Son of God."

This is the power of the Immaculate Conception. Jesus did not come through the natural seed of a fallen man. He was conceived by the Holy Ghost.

Focus on those two phrases: *Come upon thee* and *overshadow thee*. This is something you have to meditate on deeply. To be overshadowed by the power of the Highest means that God's presence completely dominates your life. It means your own thinking, your own talking, and your own acting are taken over by the Almighty. You are completely yielded. You are not thinking about your own selfish ambition; you are fully submitted to the preeminent will of God.

Mary was "good ground" for the Holy Spirit. She did not live in a cursing, toxic environment. She guarded her heart. Proverbs 4:23 commands us, *"Keep thy heart with all diligence; for out of it are the issues of life."*

You birth life from your heart! You cannot be good ground for the Holy Ghost if you are constantly watching ungodly movies, listening to worldly music, and hanging around people who speak curses. You have to guard your heart. You cannot let the filth of this world follow you into your sleep or infect your conversations.

If you want the Holy Ghost to overshadow you, you must repudiate the curses of the enemy and actively accept the blessings of God. You need to make a declaration today: "I release from my life every thought, word, or deed that was not confirmed or initiated by God Almighty! I drive it out in the name of the Lord! And I receive every prophetic word, every promise of Scripture that relates to my destiny and my character."

When the Holy Spirit overshadows you, you birth truth. You birth love. You birth the qualities of heaven. Is your womb—your spiritual capacity—good ground to carry holiness? Are you creating an environment in your home where the Spirit of God can come down and overshadow your marriage?

The Power to Name and Populate the Heavens

There is a fascinating shift that happens between the legacy of Eve and the legacy of Mary. Remember the principle of the created order: the one who names carries the responsibility.

In Genesis, Adam named all the animals. Adam named his wife. Adam was given the authority to define the creation. Even after the fall, when Eve named Cain and Abel, it was a sign of disorder because Adam had dropped his responsibility.

But look at what the angel commands Mary in Luke 1:31: *"And shalt call his name Jesus."*

Joseph did not name Jesus. The angel told Mary to name Him! She was an awesome, chosen vessel of God, and she was given the divine authority to name the Savior of the world. This marks a massive redemptive shift. Eve populated the earth with a husband, but Mary populated the heavens through the overshadowing of the Holy Ghost!

Jesus is the Last Adam. The First Adam failed, bringing sin and death to the natural world. But the Last Adam succeeded, bringing righteousness and eternal life to the spiritual world. Jesus completely overcame Adam's failures with His perfect obedience.

Through the preaching of the Gospel, Jesus is doing right now what God did in the beginning. God brought Adam into the world by speaking the Word: "Let us make man." Today, Christ brings people into the Kingdom by the power of the Word! When a person repents of their sins and gets born again, they are born into the realm of heaven.

We are filling up the heavenlies! That is the mission of the Church. We are not just making church members; we are birthing children of God. Every time you witness to a lost soul, every time you pray someone into the Kingdom, you are participating in the redemptive legacy of Mary. You are helping to populate the heavens!

Nothing Shall Be Impossible

Gabriel gives Mary another piece of revelation to build her faith. He tells her about her relative, Elizabeth. People called Elizabeth barren. She was old, well past the years of childbearing. But the angel announces that Elizabeth is already six months pregnant with a son!

God will often show you what He is doing in someone else's life to prove that He can do the miraculous in yours. Are you good ground for God to share His secrets with you? Mary was. She received the word.

Then Gabriel delivers one of the most powerful, foundation-shaking statements in the entire Bible. Luke 1:37 says: *"For with God nothing shall be impossible."*

Do you have that mentality? Do you wake up every morning and attack your day with the absolute conviction that with God, nothing shall be impossible?

If you stay with God, if you stay anchored in His Word, if you keep your spirit right, and if you yield completely to the Holy Ghost, you will break every limitation the world tries to place on you. The word of God will never fail! God's promises are eternal. They do not depend on the economy. They do not depend on the political climate. They depend entirely on the character of the Creator, and He cannot lie.

Mary's response in verse 38 is the ultimate posture of a kingmaker: *"Behold the handmaid of the Lord; be it unto me according to thy word."*

She surrendered her body, her reputation, and her future to the word of God. She aligned her life completely with heaven's purpose. That is the mentality that brings heaven down to earth.

The Standard of Sacrificial Love in Marriage

Now, we have to bring this redemptive power directly into your home. The reality of God's design must be lived out in the covenant of marriage.

If we carry the nature of God, we have to act like God. God is constantly responsible for His creation. He never gets tired. He neither slumbers nor sleeps. God is managing the entire universe with perfect love and perfect attention. Because you are born again, you carry that same divine nature!

Eternity Training Even When You're Tired

In the next world, we will be responsible for governing creation. So why would you come home from work, drop your responsibilities, and stretch out on the couch? You are in eternity training. You are responsible for your home.

Marriage requires a staggering level of love. Ephesians 5:25 commands: *"Husbands, love your wives, even as Christ also loved the church, and gave himself for it."* And Ephesians 5:28 adds: *"So ought men to love their wives as their own bodies. He that loveth his wife loveth himself."*

This goes all the way back to Genesis 2, when Adam said, "This is bone of my bones, and flesh of my flesh." To mistreat your wife is to mistreat your own body. To neglect her is to neglect yourself.

Love Requires Sacrifice

Christ's love for the Church goes deeper than basic care. Christ loves the Church sacrificially. He gave Himself for her. He laid down His life so she could be presented holy and without blemish.

Men, you cannot love your wife as Christ loves the Church without giving up something of yourself. It requires sacrifice. It requires doing things you wouldn't normally do. True love is as strong as death; it costs you something!

Study Your Wife to Love Her

You have to know your wife deeply. Because the woman came from the man in the original creation, no man is ever allowed to say, “I just don't understand my wife.” That is a cop-out! You sleep with her, you live with her, you are in a holy covenant with her—you must study her! You have to find out her tendencies, what she loves, and what brings her joy. You have to treat her according to the knowledge of God.

I tell my wife, “I am going to blow your mind.” And she will playfully say, “Have you done that yet?” But listen to me, I am absolutely committed to blowing her mind with the love of Christ.

Do you know what blowing her mind looks like? It is looking at her with pure, godly admiration. It is writing her letters. I never used to write letters, but I write letters to my wife because I love her! I study what pleases her, as long as it aligns with the standard of the Bible, and I do it.

Secretly Blowing Her Mind

Do we realize all that God does for us in secret? Do we fully appreciate how God is constantly blowing our minds behind the scenes, protecting us, blessing us, and setting up our future? That is exactly how a husband must operate for his wife. You do things for her when she doesn't see it, just as much as when she does.

Birthing Eternal Purpose

From Eve to Mary, we see the sweeping arc of God's redemptive love. Eve brought us into the physical world, but she also passed down the brokenness of the Fall. Mary, yielding entirely to the Holy Spirit, brought the Savior into the world, opening the door for us to be born again into the heavenly realm.

You are called to live with the same surrendered, faithful, pure heart that Mary demonstrated. You are called to be good ground. You are called to let the Holy Spirit overshadow your life, your marriage, and your family.

Stop settling for a merely natural existence. Stop focusing entirely on populating the earth with your physical seed, or securing earthly comfort, and start focusing on populating the heavens! Bring people to Christ. Love your spouse with a fierce, redemptive love. Walk in the Spirit so that you do not fulfill the lusts of the flesh.

When you align your life with the Word of God, when you cast down the lies of the enemy, and when you recognize the greatness God has placed inside of you, you will see the miraculous. You will look at the impossible situations in your family, your health, or your finances, and you will declare with absolute authority: "With God, nothing shall be impossible!" Let God use you to birth His purposes in this generation. Step into your redemptive legacy today.

Questions for Meditation

1. Have I been living solely with an "Eve" mindset—focusing only on my earthly legacy and natural circumstances—or am I cultivating a "Mary"

mindset, actively participating in populating the heavens?

2. Is my heart currently "good ground" for the Holy Spirit to overshadow me, or do I need to aggressively repudiate negative influences, worldly entertainment, and words of cursing from my life?

3. In what specific ways am I allowing the Holy Spirit to dominate my thoughts, my speech, and my actions so that I can birth God's truth into my generation?

4. Husbands: Am I sacrificially loving my wife the way Christ loves the Church? What is one specific, unseen sacrifice I can make this week to "blow her mind" and bless her?

5. Wives: Am I fully yielded to the Word of God like Mary was? Do I look at my children and my family through the lens of God's redemptive greatness, rather than settling for worldly labels?

Call to Action

Yield completely to the Holy Spirit just as Mary did. Purge your life of ungodly influences, guard your heart with all diligence, and allow God to use your life, your marriage, and your parenting to birth redemptive, eternal purposes in your generation. Make the deliberate choice today to love sacrificially, lead responsibly, and operate with the unwavering faith that with God, nothing shall be impossible!

Chapter 7

Overshadowed by Holiness: Mary's Character and Destiny

When you look at the story of Mary, the mother of Jesus, with eyes of revelation, you have to set aside the traditional, passive imagery the world has handed you. Mary's story is not just a nice little tale for Christmas Eve services. It is not just a manger scene on a Christmas card.

Mary's story is about fierce faith, radical obedience, and stepping boldly into a divine destiny that would shake the foundations of heaven and earth.

Mary is the redemptive woman. She is the "New Eve."

Where the first Eve, after the Fall, became the mother of a fallen creation, Mary was handpicked by Almighty God to carry the Son of God and reverse the curse! She was a vessel of holiness. When you understand the character of Mary and the destiny she fulfilled, it will challenge you to the core of your being. It will force you to ask yourself: Am I stepping into the eternal purposes God has for me? Am I living as a vessel of His presence, or am I settling for the comfort and complacency of the fallen world?

Embrace Your Divine Purpose

God is calling you higher. He is calling you to reflect His image, to carry His authority, and to participate in His eternal plan. Just as Mary embraced her divine purpose, you are called to arise, stop resisting, and live out the absolute amazement God has ordained for your life.

To fully comprehend the magnitude of Mary's calling, we have to look back at the original created order. We have to look at how God designed the family and the purpose of a woman.

In Genesis 5:1-2, the Word of God lays down a foundational truth about unity and destiny:

> *"In the day that God created man, in the likeness of God made he him; Male and female created he them; and blessed them, and called their name Adam, in the day when they were created."*

Daughter of Eve Overshadowed by Holiness

But thousands of years later, God chose another woman. A woman who would not bow to the serpent. A woman whose character, purity, and spiritual competency were so incredibly high that she qualified to carry the holiness of God Himself. She was a daughter of Eve physically, but spiritually, she was entirely different. She would carry the Savior who redeemed man from sin—the offense against God that entered the world in the Garden.

An Angelic Announcement, a Standard of Purity

Look closely at the Scripture in Luke chapter 1. This is one of the most powerful encounters in the entire Bible.

> *"In the sixth month of Elizabeth's pregnancy, God sent the angel Gabriel to Nazareth, a village in Galilee, to a virgin named Mary. She was engaged to be married to a man named Joseph, a descendant of King David" (Luke 1:26-27, NLT).*

God sends Gabriel—an archangel, a heavy hitter in the courts of heaven. This is the same Gabriel who appeared to the prophet Daniel in the Old Testament. When Daniel saw Gabriel, the power and presence of the angel were so intense that Daniel was completely undone; he fell on his face and lost all his strength. But God sends this same mighty angel to a young woman in a village called Nazareth.

Notice the specific qualifications the Bible highlights about Mary. Gabriel greets her by identifying five distinct, powerful qualities:

- She was a virgin.
- She was engaged to Joseph, a descendant of King David.
- An angel of the Lord appeared to her directly.
- She was called a "favored woman."
- The Lord was with her.

She was a virgin. The modern world desperately needs to hear this. The Bible specifically notes that Mary was a virgin. In today's culture, people mock purity. The world dismisses virginity as old-fashioned or unnecessary. Even in the church, standards have fallen. But listen. God chose a virgin to bring the Savior into the world because purity is deeply connected to spiritual destiny.

Purity is not just about keeping a set of religious rules; it is about preparing your vessel for the Holy Ghost. And this is not just for women! Men, you are not supposed to be out there having sex before you get married, either. You are supposed to be a virgin when you stand at the altar. Purity is not based on your feelings or your fleshly urges; it is based on the eternal destiny God has placed on your life.

We must make this a priority in our families again. Teach your sons and daughters to value purity. Look at your teenagers and say, "Do not have sex before you get married. Keep yourself pure. Stay focused on God." If you do not make purity a serious issue in your home, the world will gladly step in and teach them how to compromise. You must pray with your children, read the Word together, and build a culture of holiness in your house.

Mary's virginity was a testament to her character. She did not let the corruption of the world enter her body or her spirit. She guarded her heart with all diligence, and because she was pure, she found favor with the Creator of the universe.

Prophetic Declarations of Gabriel Over Mary

When Gabriel speaks to Mary, he releases an avalanche of prophetic destiny over her life. I have gone through Luke 1 and identified 21 prophetic declarations that the angel spoke over Mary. These declarations completely reverse the curse of the Fall. They are words of pure, unadulterated redemption.

Look at Gabriel's greeting in Luke 1:28: *"Greetings, favored woman! The Lord is with you!"*

Luke 1:29 says, *"Confused and disturbed, Mary tried to think what the angel could mean."*

This is amazing. Think about her spiritual strength! Daniel could not even stand up under the presence of this angel, but this young woman stands there, composed, trying to process the revelation. God gave her the ability to stand in the presence of an archangel and listen. She was that clear in her spirit.

Gabriel continues in verses 30 through 33: *"Don't be afraid, Mary," the angel told her, "for you have found favor with God! You will conceive and give birth to a son, and you will name him Jesus. He will be very great and will be called the Son of the Most High. The Lord God will give him the throne of his ancestor David. And he will reign over Israel forever; his Kingdom will never end!"*

Look at the weight of what is being spoken over her!

- "You have found favor with God."
- "You will conceive."
- "You will give birth to a son."
- "He will be very great."
- "He will be called the Son of the Most High."
- "The Lord God will give him the throne of his ancestor David."
- "He will reign over Israel forever."
- "His Kingdom will never end!"

Every one of these statements is an explosive, eternal promise. The never-ending Kingdom! Eve's kingdom was temporary. Eve's legacy was physical, and the physical life ends. But Mary was chosen to birth the eternal, spiritual Kingdom that will reign forever! She was bringing forth the Last Adam, the One who would take on the failures of the first Adam and redeem all of mankind.

The Authority to Name

Do not miss the incredible shift in authority that happens in Luke 1:31. The angel tells Mary:

> *"You will conceive and give birth to a son, and you will name him Jesus."*

In the original created order, the man was given the authority to name. Adam named the animals. Adam named his wife. The power to name is the power to define responsibility and destiny. But because Adam abdicated his leadership in the garden, the earth grew in irresponsibility.

Now, in the redemptive timeline, God bypasses the fallen order and speaks directly to the redemptive woman. Joseph did not name Jesus. The angel looked directly at Mary and said, "You will name him Jesus."

This marks a profound shift. She was given the authority to name the Son of God! Ever since Mary named Jesus, women have been participating in the spiritual naming and defining of the generations. Yes, the legacy still flows through the man's family name, but Mary's obedience restored a level of spiritual authority to the woman that had been lost in the garden. She qualified because she carried all the characteristics necessary to reverse the mistakes of Eve.

Overshadowed by the Holy Ghost

Mary asks a very practical question in verse 34:

> *"How can this happen? I am a virgin."*

She is not doubting God; she is simply asking for the mechanics of the miracle. Gabriel's answer in verse 35 is one of the most astonishing verses in all of Scripture:

> *"The angel replied, 'The Holy Spirit will come upon you, and the power of the Most High will overshadow you. So the baby to be born will be holy, and he will be called the Son of God.'"*

Meditate on those two phrases: *come upon you* and *overshadow you.*

To be overshadowed by the Holy Spirit means that God takes complete dominance over your life. When the Most High overshadows you, you are no longer thinking your own thoughts. You are no longer pursuing your own selfish ambitions. Your flesh is completely subdued, and the preeminent, dominant force in your life is the Holy Ghost.

There is a place in God where you stop thinking about yourself entirely! That is what most believers need right now. You need the Holy Ghost to come upon you and overshadow you so that your thinking, your talking, and your actions are entirely dictated by Almighty God. When you are overshadowed by Him, you birth truth. You birth destiny. You birth love.

The angel says, *"So the baby to be born will be holy."* Mary had a womb prepared to carry holiness. Her character, her purity, and her spiritual environment made her good ground.

Is your life good ground for holiness? What are you birthing in your daily life? Are you birthing the fruit of the Spirit, or are you birthing the chaos of the flesh? You cannot be overshadowed by the Holy Spirit if you are constantly filling your mind with the garbage of this world. You have to guard your heart with all diligence, for out of it flow the issues of life! You must repudiate the curses, the negativity, and the worldly entertainment that try to pollute your spirit. You have to say, "I release from me every thought, word, or deed that was not confirmed or initiated by God Almighty! And I receive every prophetic word, every Scripture that relates to my divine destiny!"

Going Up vs. Asking God to Come Down

We need to address a massive misunderstanding in the modern church regarding the presence of God. So many believers go into a church service, the worship band starts playing, the lights go down, and people start crying out, "Oh God, come down! God, we want You to come down! We want to feel Your presence!"

You are asking God to come down physically and show Himself to your flesh. But God's answer to that is: "I already did that! I sent My Son down to the earth! I sent the Holy Ghost down on the Day of Pentecost! I have no intention of trying to appeal to your flesh again. I already came down; now I am trying to get you to COME UP!" God is saying, "I never left you! I am already here! But you are not where you are supposed to be, and that is why you don't see Me!"

We think that if we sing the right song and create the right emotional atmosphere, we can manipulate God into showing up. But God is calling us to function in the eternal dimension. He didn't send the Holy Ghost just to give you a nicer house, a better job, or temporary material comforts. He sent the Holy Ghost to transform you into His image!

You are born again into a new world order. Stop asking God to cater to your natural comfort and start ascending in the Spirit. The Bible commands us to walk in the Spirit, and we will not fulfill the lust of the flesh. Walking in the Spirit means coming up to His level. It means acknowledging every good thing that is in you in Christ Jesus.

The devil resists God but believers should never resist Him, yet we resist transformation. We resist the call to holiness. We resist the demand to change.

We must return to the fear of God! The fear of God is not a natural terror; it is a deep, reverent honor that compels you to become everything God ordained you to be. It is being afraid to disobey Him. It is being afraid to entertain ungodly thoughts. It is a burning desire to please the Creator in every single aspect of your life.

I Am the Lord's Servant

When Gabriel finishes laying out this massive, impossible, world-changing prophecy, how does Mary respond? Does she panic? Does she look for an excuse? Does she worry about what the neighbors will say?

Look at her glorious response in Luke 1:38 (NLT): *"Mary responded, 'I am the Lord's servant. May everything you have said about me come true.'"*

Go, girl! Goodness gracious alive! What a statement of absolute surrender!

Women, can you say that right now? "I am the Lord's servant." When is the last time you said that when you were facing a trial? When is the last time you said that in relation to a husband who wasn't acting right? In relation to a boss who overlooked you for a promotion? In relation to a teacher who treated you unfairly?

Most wives know they are called to serve their husbands, but true submission is rooted in serving the Lord. When a wife submits to her husband, she is saying, "I am the Lord's servant." You do not serve people based on whether they deserve it; you serve them because you are living your life before God!

David understood this. When he repented, he cried out to God in Psalm 51, *"Against thee, thee only, have I sinned."* You live your life before God, and you live your life for the eternal rewards He will give you. You stay godly during the trial. You maintain your holiness when the pressure is on.

Mary said, *"May everything you have said about me come true."* She completely embraced the Word of God. She didn't argue. She didn't doubt. She simply agreed with heaven.

This is exactly what you are to do. Go to the Bible and see what the Lord has said about you. Stop focusing on what the world says about you. Stop dwelling on the criticisms of your enemies, or the failures of your past, or the limitations of your bank account. Your biggest problem is that you do not know what the Lord has said about you, and you do not emphasize His Word enough.

Go through the Scriptures. Underline every promise. Circle every verse that relates to your destiny. Eat the Word of God as your daily food. Stand up like Mary and declare:

"May everything You have revealed to me be reality! May every promise You have spoken over my life come true!"

Rise Above Everything to Be Like God

God wants to amaze you. He cannot be anything else but amazing. Ephesians 3:20 says He is able to do exceedingly abundantly above all that we ask or think, according to the power that works in us. But what He can release into your life depends entirely on where you let Him take you and how much you are willing to grow.

Mary was just a young woman from a humble village, but she did not let her background dictate her future. You might come from a broken family. You might have faced rejection. I only saw my biological father twice in my entire life! But you cannot let the limitations of your past, or the lies of the enemy, determine your destiny. Rise up above the devil's lies. Rise above false prophecies, criticisms, and fleshly insecurities. The world will try to present so much negativity that you receive it and allow others to determine your future. But God has your future in His hands.

Do you know how beautiful God made you? When God formed you, He made you awesome. Stop looking at your flaws or your perceived shortcomings. Get God's viewpoint of yourself. You are highly favored. You are designed to conceive eternal things, just as Mary conceived Jesus.

You have angels working around you right now. Just as Gabriel appeared to Mary, and Michael fought for Daniel, there are angels operating in the unseen realm to glorify God and to bless your life. Stay aligned with the Holy Spirit and say, "I am the Lord's servant."

Do not settle for a natural existence. You are called to a heavenly legacy. You are called to be overshadowed by the holiness of God. Allow the Holy Ghost to dominate your thoughts, your marriage, and your family. Step into the eternal dimension, walk in the fear of God, and let the transforming power of Jesus Christ shine through you for the whole world to see!

Questions for Meditation

1. Am I stepping into the eternal purposes God has for me?
2. Am I living as a vessel of His presence, or am I settling for comfort and complacency?
3. In what areas of my life am I resisting the Holy Spirit's desire to "overshadow" and dominate my thoughts and actions?
4. How does understanding Mary's radical obedience ("I am the Lord's servant") change the way I view submission and service in my own difficult circumstances?
5. What do you believe is God's purpose for your life? What steps can you take today to align with God's purpose for your life?

Call to Action

It's time to stop resisting and start reflecting His image. Let's honor God by becoming everything He's created us to be. Determine today to guard your heart, pursue absolute purity, and embrace the eternal destiny God has spoken over you. Stop asking God to "come down" to your comfort level, and instead boldly step up into the spiritual dimension He has prepared for you. Declare today: "I am the Lord's servant; let it be to me according to Your Word!"

Chapter 8

Transforming Power and Christlike Character

God is perfecting us, and I want to declare something to you right now so it gets deep into your spirit: the devil is not winning! You are made to win in life, period. We look around at the world today, and it is easy to get discouraged. We see the culture sliding, we see families under attack, and we see people trading the eternal truth of God for temporary, fleshly satisfaction. But you cannot let the condition of the fallen world dictate the condition of your spirit. The devil is a defeated foe, running around with his tail between his legs. He knows his time is short, but he is terrified of a believer who actually knows who they are in Christ.

God did not leave us down here to just survive. He did not save you so you could barely hang on until the rapture. Jesus sent the Holy Ghost to make you conscious of the fact that you are cultivating a powerful, victorious spirituality. True transformation is not about holding a title in a church. It is about living in the image of Christ every single day. The world is absolutely desperate for light. People are starving for something real. They do not need more religious clichés or fleeting political solutions. They need to see the transforming power of the living God operating in a human being.

You are called to walk in Christlike integrity. You are called to embody the love, grace, and truth of the Savior. This is about bringing God's kingdom to earth and becoming the unmistakable light in your home, your city, and your generation. Let us not settle for merely being "good" people. Let us pursue true, radical transformation through the power of the Holy Spirit. The goal is far more than just making it to heaven after you die; it is about living in His kingdom authority here and now.

The Original Order and the Eternal Mindset

To understand the magnitude of the transforming power inside of you, we have to go back to the blueprint. We have to look at the original order of creation. When you understand how God made things in the beginning, you will understand how He operates in the new creation today.

Look at Genesis 2:19. The Word of God says:

> *"And out of the ground the Lord God formed every beast of the field, and every fowl of the air; and brought them unto Adam to see what he would call them: and whatsoever Adam called every living creature, that was the name thereof."*

Now, I want you to read that carefully and think about the creative power of God. You probably wouldn't normally think about it this way, but God made the animals fully grown. He didn't form eggs and wait for them to hatch. He didn't form little baby cubs or helpless infants that had to be nursed in the wild. Out of the ground, the Lord God formed every beast of the field, and He brought them straight to Adam to be named.

There is a profound creative order and pattern here. When God makes a man, He makes a man. When God makes a woman, He makes a woman. Yes, later there would be the marriage bed, conception, gestation, and birth for humanity. But the original creations came forth fully formed by the spoken word and the handiwork of Almighty God. They followed a specific order.

And here is the reality you must grasp: everything that God made originally was made to live forever! Man was not created to be a sweaty, exhausted farmer toiling in the dirt just to survive. God placed the man in the garden to eat the fruit, to commune with the Creator, and to be like God. He did not have to eat to live.

This is incredibly important for you to understand as you prepare for eternity. Do you think that in the next world, when you have eternal life, you are going to have to eat a meal just to stay alive? By definition, that is a nonsense question! You have eternal life! You are going to live forever! So that means, even back in the garden, eating off the trees was not a desperate requirement for survival. You don't need food that way when you are an eternal being.

The eternal God does not need food. He does not get hungry. He does not get tired. And His children, created in His image and restored to eternal life, do not need physical sustenance to maintain their existence. In the next world, eating is optional. It is a joy, it is a fellowship, but it is not a necessity. You will live off the substance of the essence of what you are made out of! You are not merely a time and space being.

You use time and space right now, but you are not limited by them.

Meditate on this! When you get your rewards in heaven, you are not going to have to scramble for food because you are sealed by the Holy Ghost of promise. You have eternal life pulsating through your very being.

Meat You Know Not Of

If physical food is not the ultimate sustenance for an eternal being, then what is? We find the answer in the redemptive life of Jesus Christ.

When Jesus was ministering to the woman at the well in John 4, His disciples went away to buy food. They came back and urged Him to eat. But Jesus looked at them and said, "I have meat to eat that ye know not of." The disciples were confused. They thought someone else had brought Him a sandwich. But Jesus clarified His statement with a principle that should completely revolutionize how you live your life.

He said, "My meat is to do the will of Him that sent me, and to finish His work."

Listen to me! When you are born again, the spiritual food that is inside of you right now will always be the food you live by. Jesus was in a physical body, but He declared that doing the will of God was His actual nourishment. When the disciples wanted Him to eat temporal food, He was already feasting on divine revelation. His purpose was His food. His responsibility was His sustenance!

In eternity, whatever there is to do will be the will of God. That means the principles of heaven—principles that are fixed, uniform, and universal—are the actual substance of your life. Godliness is an eternal value. Righteousness is an eternal value. That is your food!

We get so caught up in the temporal constructs of this physical world. We live for the size of our house. We live for the title on our office door. We live for the money in our bank accounts. We live for our education and our worldly accolades. But let me tell you the absolute truth: that stuff is going to burn! The house is going to burn. The car is going to rust. The bank account is going to vanish.

You have to transition from temporal values to eternal values. You have to start feeding your spirit on the will of God. When you wake up in the morning, your first thought should not be, "How can I make more money today?" Your first thought should be, "Father, what is Your will for me today? Give me my daily bread, which is the assignment You have placed on my life!" That is what it means to be sustained by the meat of heaven.

The Glory of the Latter House

We have to break free from earthly thinking, even when it comes to our families and our relationships. The Bible tells us that gender and biological roles are not eternal constructs in the way we understand them now. I live on the fact that God made me a man in this life. I cannot change that, and I operate in the authority of it. But in the next world, those biological structures do not govern us.

Think about the angels. One time when Gabriel appeared to Daniel, he looked like a man. God Himself spoke from a burning bush, and another time He was a still, small voice. In other words, God can take shape and form. Do you think you are going to be limited in eternity? You are made in the image of God! The potential for transformation in eternity is staggering, but you will never grasp it while you are still acting like a knucklehead living only for natural food and natural status.

Earthly hierarchies do not automatically transfer to the Kingdom of Heaven. You might be the parent of your biological children right now, and you have a holy responsibility to raise them in the fear of the Lord. But in heaven, you are not going to be their parent in the same biological hierarchy. In fact, they may prove to be far more devout than you are in this life!

In the next world, their mansion, their placement, and their eternal rewards may be way above the place you are qualified to handle. You might be able to see them or visit them, but you may not be in authority over them, because heavenly rewards are based entirely on personal devotion and faithfulness to the Creator, not on earthly family trees!

This is what the Scripture means conceptually when it says the glory of the latter house is greater than the glory of the former. The "former house" is our earthly beginning. It is the natural family structure, the temporal wealth, the things we start with. But the "latter house" is the spiritual growth, the deep devotion, and the eternal placement we step into.

If you have children who truly listen to their mother and father, and then they go into the Bible for themselves, they take your revelation and multiply it with their own personal devotion to God. Where does that take them? It takes them to a greater glory! God is the One who distributes the rewards for your devotion.

You may be able to see the great figures of history in heaven. Look at how Jesus assessed John the Baptist. He said John was the greatest prophet born of a woman. But then Jesus flipped the script and said that he who is least in the Kingdom of Heaven is greater than John! God's assessment of greatness is entirely different from man's assessment. Stop relying on human-defined measures of success! Stop worrying about who is clapping for you on earth and start living for the applause of heaven.

God's Assessment of Being Born Again

How does God assess being born again? We have turned "born again" into a religious cliché. We print it on bumper stickers and use it as a demographic category. But we do not fully understand how God sees it.

From God's perspective, being born again is the literal embodiment of the quickening Spirit inside of you. It is the miraculous reality that the Spirit of the Living God has moved into your dead, fallen spirit and quickened it—made it absolutely, vibrantly alive!

Romans 8 tells us that if the Spirit of Him that raised up Jesus from the dead dwells in you, He that raised up Christ from the dead shall also quicken your mortal bodies by His Spirit that dwells in you. That is the ability inside of you right now!

When you are truly born again and moving toward your glorified state, you become fully yielded to the Holy Ghost. You become one spirit with God. Do you know what that looks like? It means living a life with zero rebellion. It means living with zero resistance to the will of the Father. It means there is no fear, no hesitancy, and no sorrow in your spirit. All of the anxiety and dread that plague the natural man are stripped away, replaced only by the pure, unadulterated goodness that comes from the Creator of the whole world!

My God, this is amazing! When you realize the truth about who you are when you are born again, it changes everything. You stop begging God for temporary relief and start commanding your circumstances to align with your eternal identity. You stop making excuses for your flesh and start walking in the transforming power of the Spirit.

The devil wants you to think you are just a struggling sinner trying to do your best. He wants you to identify with your past, your failures, and your earthly limitations. But God's assessment of you is that you are a new creation! Old things are passed away; behold, all things are become new! You possess the quickening Spirit. You have the capacity to live free from fear. You are being prepared for eternal responsibility.

Walking in Christlike Character

If we truly believe we possess this quickening Spirit, then it must radically alter our behavior. We cannot claim to have the transforming power of God inside of us while acting just like the fallen world. The evidence of the quickening Spirit is Christlike character.

The Apostle Paul unlocks the great mystery of the gospel in Colossians 1:27:

"To whom God would make known what is the riches of the glory of this mystery among the Gentiles; which is Christ in you, the hope of glory."

Christ in you! That is the mystery! The Creator of the universe did not just write you a rulebook; He placed His own Son inside of your spirit! You are the vessel of His glory.

Walking in Christlike character means you intentionally embody the love, grace, and truth of Jesus Christ in every interaction. It means you stop reacting to people out of your flesh and start responding to them out of your spirit. When someone insults you, the flesh wants to insult them back. The flesh wants to defend its pride. But Christ in you desires to show mercy. Christ in you desires to speak life.

Integrity is not just a nice moral concept; it is the absolute baseline of Christlike character. Integrity means you are the same person in the dark that you are in the light. It means you do not cheat on your taxes, you do not lie to your spouse, and you do not cut corners at your job, because your meat is to do the will of God! You are representing the King of Kings. How dare we drag His holy name through the mud of our own selfish compromises?

We are called to serve others. Jesus washed the feet of His disciples. The King of Glory took on the form of a servant. If Christ is in you, then a servant's heart must be in you. You cannot be a kingmaker without being a servant first. Husbands, serve your wives sacrificially. Wives, serve your husbands with honor. Parents, serve your children by laying down a foundation of unwavering righteousness.

Your words have to change. The Bible says that death and life are in the power of the tongue. When you walk in Christlike character, you use your words to build up, to edify, and to prophesy destiny over people. You stop complaining about the darkness and start speaking light. You stand boldly for the truth, refusing to bow to the political correctness of a confused culture.

This is how we shift the culture of our communities. We do not shift the culture by out-arguing people on the internet. We shift the culture by out-loving them, out-serving them, and out-living them! When the world sees a man or a woman who is unbothered by temporal losses, who does not panic when the economy shakes, and who lives with profound, joyful integrity, it completely shatters their paradigm. They will look at you and wonder, "What kind of meat is this person eating?" And you will be able to look them in the eye and say, "My meat is to do the will of the Father. Christ in me is the hope of glory!"

Transition from the Temporal to the Eternal

We are in a season of transition. God is calling His people to cross over from living for the temporal to living for the eternal. The temporal world is loud. It demands your attention. It screams at you through your television, your phone, and your bank statements. It tries to convince you that your worth is tied to what you own, what you wear, and who approves of you.

But the eternal realm operates on a completely different frequency. The eternal realm measures success by obedience. It measures wealth by the depth of your revelation. It measures power by your willingness to submit to the Holy Spirit.

You have to make a choice today about which house you are building. Are you pouring all your energy into the former house—the natural, earthly, temporary existence that is destined for the fire? Or are you investing your life into the latter house—the spiritual, eternal, glorified existence that will stand forever?

Everything you do today echoes into eternity. The way you treat your family matters. The way you handle your finances matters. The secret devotions you have in your prayer closet matter. God is watching, and He is preparing to distribute rewards based on your faithfulness to His fixed, uniform, and universal principles.

Stop settling for a weak, anemic version of Christianity that only asks God to bless your natural plans. Step into the transforming power of the quickening Spirit! Allow the Holy Ghost to completely overhaul your character. Take off the filthy garments of the old man, and put on the glorious righteousness of the new man.

You were not made to live a defeated life. The devil is not winning your family. The devil is not winning your mind. The devil is not winning your future! You are of God, little children, and you have overcome them, because greater is He that is in you than he that is in the world.

Live by the will of God. Feed on the meat of heaven. Let the reality of eternal life dictate every decision you make. Embody the character of Jesus Christ and let the hope of glory shine so brightly out of your life that it transforms everyone around you. You are a kingmaker. You carry the legacy of redemption. Now walk in the power of it, and let God be glorified in everything you do!

Questions for Meditation

1. Have I been living my life fueled primarily by the temporal "food" of worldly success, or am I truly sustained by the "meat" of doing the will of God?
2. In what specific ways am I investing in the "latter house" (my eternal spiritual placement) rather than obsessing over the "former house" (my temporary earthly status)?
3. Does my daily behavior reflect God's assessment of a born-again believer—living free from rebellion, resistance, and fear, fully yielded to the quickening Spirit?
4. How does understanding that biological roles and temporal wealth will "burn" change the way I interact with my family and my career today?
5. Am I actively embodying the truth of Colossians 1:27 ("Christ in you, the hope of glory") by demonstrating Christlike integrity, service, and love in my home and community?

Call to Action

Stop relying on human-defined measures of success and temporal validation. Commit today to transition your focus entirely from the physical to the eternal. Use your words, your financial decisions, and your daily deeds to deliberately reflect Christ's character. Ask the Holy Spirit to quicken your mortal body, reject every trace of fear and rebellion, and step into your community right now as an unstoppable force of transforming light and truth!

Chapter 9

Born Again and Beyond

You were created for more than just existing in a fallen world. You were designed by Almighty God to lead, to govern, and to exercise divine dominion. It is time to stop settling for anything less than your full spiritual potential. The same Spirit that raised Jesus Christ from the dead is alive inside of you right now. He is quickening your mortal body to fulfill a holy purpose and empowering you to make earth look like heaven long before you ever get there.

Being born again is not just a ticket to escape hell. You are not just saved to survive; you are saved to transform, to lead, and to bring the authority of the Kingdom into every room you enter. When you truly grasp the magnitude of the quickening Spirit of God, it changes everything about how you live, how you prioritize your time, and how you see the world around you.

Radical Faith: Prioritizing Souls Over Possessions

Let me tell you where my heart is. Recently, my wife and I were thinking about moving down to Florida. We spent time looking for a house, and to be honest, we were very unsuccessful in finding the right one. My wife is particular about what she wants in a home, and that is fine. But I told her, I would drop this entire house hunt right now, move to Bangkok, Thailand, get a simple two-bedroom apartment, and just preach the gospel.

I am radicalized for the Kingdom of God! I told my wife that the businesses and the assets she has built are worth a lot of money, but one single soul getting saved is worth a billion times more than any earthly company. The priority of your life must go where the eternal value is.

We get so caught up in looking for the perfect house, securing the perfect retirement, and accumulating earthly possessions. But what does any of that matter if the world around us is dying and going to hell? Jesus gave us a very clear, uncompromising mandate in Matthew 24:14:

> *"And this gospel of the kingdom shall be preached in all the world for a witness unto all nations; and then shall the end come."*

The early disciples did not have the technology, the wealth, or the global infrastructure that we have today. They didn't have social media, airplanes, or massive church buildings. But they had one thing that mattered above all else: they had Jesus. They had the quickening power of the Holy Ghost, and that was enough to turn the entire world upside down.

Today, we face the same call. We must prioritize souls over our possessions. We need technically skilled people, business leaders, and everyday believers to use modern tools to push the gospel into the darkest corners of the earth. But tools mean nothing without radical faith. Revival has always started with ordinary people who said a radical "yes" to an extraordinary God.

The Sin of Ignoring God

Look at the spiritual condition of America right now. The greatest sin of this nation is the sin of ignoring God's grace. We have politicians, business leaders, and cultural influencers who know about God. We print "In God We Trust" on our currency. The foundation of this country was built on a Puritan ethic. Their sin is not complete ignorance; their sin is that they actively ignore the saving grace that is readily available to them.

Because we have prioritized power and possessions over the gospel, we are seeing the judgment of that rebellion play out in our streets. Look at the manipulation, the lies, the violence, and the absolute lack of moral sense in our culture today.

But there is an answer, and the answer is revival. Think back to the Cane Ridge and Muddy River Revivals of the early 1800s. When people expanded out West, there was lawlessness. People robbed, pillaged, and killed. There were no sheriffs to keep order. But bold pastors—Presbyterians, Methodists, and Baptists—went out into that wild frontier. They carried the fire of the Holy Ghost with them. They brought the stability of the Word of God, and Jesus went out there with them, sparking awakenings that transformed entire regions!

We need that same fire today. We need men and women who are willing to step into the lawless, chaotic spaces of modern society and establish the order of heaven.

The Power of Proximity and Influence

You might think you only have a little bit of influence. You might look at your physical limitations or your financial circumstances and assume God cannot use you to shake a nation. That is a lie from the pit of hell! Your physical condition does not dictate your spiritual authority.

I think of a woman I heard praying recently named Barbara Massie. She has been going through severe physical challenges, battling sickness in her body. But let me tell you something: the life of God inside of her is not sick at all! It does not matter how weak she might sound in her natural voice or how she feels physically. Who she is spiritually is a forever standard.

If a woman like that, armed with the absolute belief system of the Bible, walked into a nation that had never heard the gospel and declared, “Follow me as I follow Christ,” she could spark the transformation of an entire country! Why? Because Jesus owns the body she lives in. The quickening Spirit inside of her is far greater than the natural limitations of her flesh.

When you are born again, you carry the presence of the Almighty. The people around you should experience a transformative influence just by being in proximity to your devotion. You do not transform lives because of where you have been or how much money you make. You transform lives because you have become the church wherever you go!

Be the Light

Stop cursing the darkness. Stop complaining about the moral failures of the culture, the government, and even the church.

Complaining only magnifies the problem. Christlikeness solves the problem!

The world does not need more of your political opinions. It does not need more failed social solutions or empty religious clichés. The world needs light. It needs to see the life of Jesus Christ visibly demonstrated in your daily character.

The Apostle Paul reveals the ultimate secret to this transforming power in Colossians 1:27:

> *"To whom God would make known what is the riches of the glory of this mystery among the Gentiles; which is Christ in you, the hope of glory."*

Christ in you! That is the mystery that shatters the darkness. You must embody the love, grace, and truth of the Savior. Being the light is not a passive existence; it is a fiercely active calling. It means you step up and take action. You step into leadership roles at your job. You address the needs in your community. You make your neighborhood better simply because you live there.

If you want to be the light, you must live with absolute integrity. Character matters. You cannot live like the devil in private and expect to carry the authority of God in public. You must seek God with your whole heart. Jeremiah 29:13 declares, "And ye shall seek me, and find me, when ye shall search for me with all your heart." You must admit your own need for ongoing personal transformation, walking in daily repentance and a willingness to grow.

Serve the people around you. Look for opportunities to meet the needs of others through acts of kindness and bold mentorship. Speak life! Use your words to uplift, inspire, and prophesy destiny over people, rather than tearing them down with criticism. Stand unapologetically for biblical truth, even when the culture tells you it is unpopular. Cultivate a spirit of joy and gratitude, because the joy of the Lord is an infectious light that can pierce the deepest gloom.

The Quickening Spirit and True Leadership

You must understand the mechanics of what happens when you are born again. God breathes His life into you, and you become a new creation. But salvation is just the beginning. God expects you to live at the level of your spiritual birthright.

Look back at the created order in Genesis. God gave Adam the command to be fruitful, multiply, replenish the earth, and subdue it. Adam was designed to govern the garden. But when the serpent came in, Adam was irresponsible. He was not deceived; he just abdicated his leadership. He stepped aside when he should have stepped up to protect his wife and his domain.

God is calling you to take care of business in your own garden right now! Your garden is your thought life, your heart, your principles, and your family. You cannot allow the enemy to whisper lies into your home. You cannot allow the culture to dictate how you raise your children. You must step up and lead.

God has provided the infrastructure for your success: His creation, His Word, and His grace. But you have a human responsibility to draw close to Him and execute His will. Stop blaming God for the dissatisfaction in your life, and start taking responsibility for your own spiritual growth.

When you fully yield to the Holy Ghost, you open the floodgates of heaven. The Spirit quickens you. He gives you the power to do extraordinary, godly things. He gives you the vision to create industries, not just find jobs. He gives you the capacity to restore broken marriages, heal the sick, and cast out devils.

You are born again and beyond! You are a kingmaker. You carry the very nature of the Creator. Do not let the devil keep you bound by a mediocre, survival-mentality existence. Rise up, walk in the Spirit, and take your rightful place in the divine order. The world is desperately waiting for the greatness that God has placed inside of you.

Questions for Meditation

1. Am I prioritizing the eternal value of souls, or have I allowed the pursuit of earthly possessions and comfort to dominate my focus?

2. In what specific ways am I acting as a transformative light in my workplace, community, and home, rather than just complaining about the darkness?

3. How does the reality of “Christ in me, the hope of glory” change the way I approach leadership and responsibility in my daily life?

4. Are there areas in my personal “garden” (my thoughts, family, or principles) where I have stepped aside instead of stepping up to lead?

5. What steps must I take today to stop settling for spiritual survival and start living at the full level of my divine birthright?

Call to Action

Today, choose to rise. Choose to be the exact person God designed you to be from the foundation of the world. Stop relying on human-defined measures of success, and start using your words, decisions, and deeds to reflect Christ's character. Step into the dark places of your community and shift the culture by being an unstoppable vessel of light. The world is waiting for the greatness inside you—take your rightful place and lead!

Additional Resources

Your Invitation to Christ's Eternal Reign

Imagine this: the adventure of eternal life isn't some far-off dream—it's a present reality, waiting for you to embrace it. Through faith in Jesus Christ, you're invited to leave behind the limitations of this world and step into your destiny as a child of God. This is your moment to reign with Christ, to explore the infinite wonders of His kingdom, and to live in perfect harmony with His will.

Will you accept the invitation? The journey begins now, and the destination is eternal. As Jesus Himself declared, "I have come that they may have life, and have it to the full" (John 10:10). The adventure of eternal life is here—step into your destiny today.

Let's explore the grand narrative of humanity together. It's a story of creation, fall, redemption, and eternal destiny—a story that surpasses any earthly achievement. It begins with God's declaration in Genesis 1:26, where He resolved to create humanity in His image, granting both man and woman dominion over the Earth. Adam and Eve were entrusted with the task of populating and stewarding the Earth. But their failure in the Garden of Eden introduced sin and death into the world. Eve became the mother of all living sinners, while Adam's abdication of responsibility disrupted God's original design.

Then, the story shifts to Mary, the mother of Jesus. Through her obedience and faith, the Savior—the "last Adam"—was born. Jesus offers redemption and eternal life, inviting humanity to be born again. This rebirth isn't for earthly dominion but for the heavenly realm. Through spiritual transformation, believers become children of God, destined to reign with Christ in His eternal kingdom.

Revelation 5:10 and 2 Timothy 2:12 reveal the promise of reigning with Christ forever, with responsibilities in the new heaven and new earth. Consider the contrast: the earthly legacy of Eve's children, marked by sin and mortality, versus the heavenly legacy of Mary's spiritual children, characterized by righteousness and eternal life.

Living with an eternal perspective changes everything. It prepares you for the responsibilities of the heavenly realm and allows you to embrace the transformative power of being born again. This is your opportunity to participate in the ultimate adventure—a journey where you fulfill your divine purpose, reign with Christ, and explore the infinite wonders of God's kingdom.

Forget space missions and earthly accolades—there's a greater journey calling you. From the creation of Adam and Eve to the redemption brought by Jesus Christ, humanity's story is the ultimate adventure of purpose, redemption, and eternal destiny.

Through faith in Jesus, you're invited to be born again—not just for this world, but for the heavenly realm. Imagine reigning with Christ forever, exploring the infinite wonders of God's kingdom, and fulfilling your divine purpose.

"You have made them to be a kingdom and priests to serve our God, and they will reign on the earth." (Revelation 5:10)

This is your invitation to step into a life of eternal significance. The adventure begins now. Will you accept it?

Exploring Your Eternal Journey

A Discussion Guide for Deeper Reflection

Welcome to a journey of discovery and reflection—a guide designed to deepen your understanding of the eternal narrative presented in *Kingmaker Power: The Legacy of Two Kingmakers* by Wellington Boone.

This outline serves as a framework for group discussions, personal study, or teaching sessions, inviting you to explore the profound truths of humanity's creation, fall, redemption, and eternal destiny.

Through this guide, you'll trace the story of Adam and Eve's earthly dominion, the redemptive role of Mary and her Son, Jesus Christ, and the ultimate calling of believers to reign with Christ in the eternal realm. Each section is crafted to spark meaningful conversations and inspire a deeper connection to your divine purpose.

Whether you're gathering with others or reflecting on your own, this outline will help you unpack the rich themes of the book, offering insights into God's design for humanity and the eternal adventure that awaits. Let this be more than a study—let it be an invitation to step into your destiny as a child of God.

Your Eternal Journey: From Earthly Dominion to Heavenly Reign

Part 1: The Earthly Dominion of Adam and Eve

1. The Creation Mandate

Genesis 1:26-28: "Let us make man in our image, after our likeness, and let them have dominion... Be fruitful and multiply, and replenish the earth, and subdue it."

Adam and Eve were created in God's image, reflecting His nature and authority.

Their mission was to populate the Earth, steward creation, and live in harmony with God's design.

2. Adam's Responsibility and Failure

Genesis 2:15: "The LORD God placed the man in the Garden of Eden to tend and watch over it." Adam was given the responsibility to lead, protect, and maintain the created order.

Genesis 3:6: Adam's failure to protect the garden and his wife led to the fall of humanity.

1 Timothy 2:14: "And it was not Adam who was deceived, but the woman being deceived fell into transgression."

Adam's abdication of responsibility allowed sin to enter the world, fracturing the created order.

3. Eve: The Mother of All Living

Genesis 3:20: "Adam named his wife Eve, because she would be the mother of all who live."

Eve's legacy is one of physical life, as her descendants populated the Earth.

However, all her children were born in sin, inheriting the fallen nature of Adam (Romans 5:12).

Part 2: The Heavenly Reign of Mary's Spiritual Children

1. Mary: The Mother of Redemption

Luke 1:30-31: "Do not be afraid, Mary; you have found favor with God. You will conceive and give birth to a son, and you are to call him Jesus."

Mary, a descendant of Eve, was chosen to bear the Savior, Jesus Christ, who would redeem humanity.

Unlike Eve, who brought physical life, Mary's role was to bring spiritual life through her Son.

2. Jesus: The Last Adam

1 Corinthians 15:45: "The first man Adam became a living being; the last Adam, a life-giving spirit."

Jesus is the prototype of the new creation, showing humanity how to live in alignment with God's will.

Through His death and resurrection, He made it possible for humanity to be born again and restored to God's image.

3. Born Again for the Realm of Heaven

John 3:3: "Unless one is born again, he cannot see the kingdom of God."

Spiritual rebirth is the gateway to eternal life and participation in God's heavenly kingdom.

Philippians 3:20-21: "Our citizenship is in heaven, and we eagerly await a Savior from there, the Lord Jesus Christ, who... will transform our lowly bodies so that they will be like His glorious body."

Those born again are no longer bound by earthly limitations but are destined for eternal glory.

Part 3: Reigning with Christ in the Eternal Realm

1. The Promise of Eternal Reign

Revelation 5:10: "You have made them to be a kingdom and priests to serve our God, and they will reign on the earth."

Believers are called to reign with Christ, exercising authority in the new heaven and new earth.

2 Timothy 2:12: "If we endure, we will also reign with Him."

Faithfulness in this life prepares believers for their eternal responsibilities.

2. The Heavenly Kingdom

Revelation 21:1-4: "Then I saw a new heaven and a new earth... God's dwelling place is now among the people, and He will dwell with them."

The new creation will be a place of perfect harmony, where God's people will live and reign forever.

Revelation 22:5: "They will reign forever and ever."

The reign of believers is eternal, reflecting God's original design for humanity to have dominion.

3. Responsibilities in the Eternal Realm

Luke 19:17: "Well done, my good servant! Because you have been trustworthy in a very small matter, take charge of ten cities."

Believers' faithfulness on Earth determines their responsibilities in the eternal kingdom.

1 Corinthians 6:3: "Do you not know that we will judge angels?"

The redeemed will have authority not only over creation but also in the spiritual realm.

Part 4: The Contrast Between Earthly and Heavenly Realms

1. Earthly Dominion: The Legacy of Eve

Eve's children populated the Earth but inherited sin and death (Romans 5:12).

Their reign was limited to the physical realm and marred by the consequences of the fall.

2. Heavenly Reign: The Legacy of Mary

Mary's spiritual children, born again through faith in Jesus, are destined to populate the heavens.

Their reign is eternal, characterized by righteousness, peace, and joy in the Holy Spirit (Romans 14:17).

3. The Eternal Perspective

Colossians 3:1-2: "Set your minds on things above, not on earthly things."

Believers are called to live with an eternal perspective, focusing on their heavenly destiny.

Matthew 6:19-20: "Do not store up for yourselves treasures on earth... but store up for yourselves treasures in heaven."

Earthly achievements are temporary, but heavenly rewards are eternal.

Part 5: The Adventure of Eternal Life

1. Training for Eternity

Hebrews 12:1-2: "Let us run with perseverance the race marked out for us, fixing our eyes on Jesus."

Life on Earth is preparation for the responsibilities of eternity.

Ephesians 2:10: "For we are God's handiwork, created in Christ Jesus to do good works, which God prepared in advance for us to do."

Believers are called to live out their divine purpose, reflecting God's glory.

2. The Glory of the Latter House

Haggai 2:9: "The glory of this latter house shall be greater than of the former."

The spiritual children of Mary, born again through Jesus, will surpass the earthly legacy of Eve's children.

John 14:2-3: "In My Father's house are many mansions... I go to prepare a place for you."

Jesus is preparing an eternal home for His followers, where they will dwell with Him forever.

3. The Eternal Adventure

Isaiah 9:7: "Of the increase of His government and peace there will be no end."

The reign of Christ and His people will expand eternally, exploring the infinite creativity of God.

1 Corinthians 2:9: "No eye has seen, no ear has heard, and no mind has imagined what God has prepared for those who love Him."

The eternal realm will be a place of endless discovery, joy, and fulfillment.

www.ingramcontent.com/pod-product-compliance
Lightning Source LLC
LaVergne TN
LVHW010928110826
845149LV00013B/2517

* 9 7 8 0 9 9 7 4 7 1 0 2 1 *